RUDOLF STEINER (1861–1925) called his spiritual philosophy 'anthroposophy', meaning 'wisdom of the human being'. As a highly developed seer, he based his work on direct knowledge and perception of spiritual dimensions. He initiated a modern and universal 'science of spirit', accessible to anyone willing to exercise clear and unprejudiced thinking.

From his spiritual investigations Steiner provided suggestions for the renewal of many activities, including education (both general and special), agriculture, medicine, economics, architecture, science, philosophy, religion and the arts. Today there are thousands of schools, clinics, farms and other organizations involved in practical work based on his principles. His many published works feature his research into the spiritual nature of the human being, the evolution of the world and humanity, and methods of personal development. Steiner wrote some 30 books and delivered over 6000 lectures across Europe. In 1924 he founded the General Anthroposophical Society, which today has branches throughout the world.

MUSIC

Mystery, Art and the Human Being

RUDOLF STEINER

Edited and Introduced by Michael Kurtz

Translated from German by Matthew Barton

RUDOLF STEINER PRESS

Rudolf Steiner Press,
Hillside House, The Square
Forest Row, RH18 5ES

www.rudolfsteinerpress.com

Published by Rudolf Steiner Press 2016

Originally published in German under the title *Die Welt der Musik* by Rudolf Steiner Verlag, Basel, in 2012

A catalogue record for this book is available from the British Library

Print book ISBN: 978 1 85584 526 8
Ebook ISBN: 978 1 85584 481 0

Cover by Morgan Creative. Cover image © Frog-travel
Typeset by DP Photosetting, Neath, West Glamorgan
Printed and bound by 4Edge Ltd., Essex

CONTENTS

INTRODUCTION

'The true nature of music, the spiritual element in music, is found between the tones, lies in the intervals as an inaudible quality.'[1]

From the ancient, sophisticated cultures of the East through Greek antiquity to medieval Christianity in Europe, music has always played a natural and clearly defined role in many forms of ritual, worship and education. In past eras people still felt there to be concord between music, humanity and the world of stars, which was regarded as the dwelling place of the gods. But that time has passed. Nowadays our view of music has sundered itself from these general religious outlooks, and the classical modes of, say, Bach, Beethoven or Bruckner, have become just one idiom amongst many other possibilities. Today every composer has their own distinct view of music.

What is the reason for this change of outlook? A signature of the modern age is that people release themselves from traditions and prescribed rules, instead taking autonomous, individual decisions and actions. In a questionnaire Rudolf Steiner once completed in Weimar in 1893, he coined the phrase 'The free human being in place of God' as his personal motto.[2] This emancipatory process is still in its birth pangs, but is certainly a feature of daily contemporary life.

Born three years after the end of the Second World War, I have always felt an interest in the cultural atmosphere of those post-war years. It was a time of reflection, of sober assessment after the horrors of the war, and in the arts led to a radical new beginning but at the same time also to an imaginatively impoverished 'material art'. At the time two small works threw open the doors to literally radical new developments; going to the very root of things they sought to start again from zero. These were two experiments that made history by helping to dismantle the final vestiges of tradition. In Cologne, at the 'Electronic Studio', Karlheinz Stockhausen composed his *Study I* in 1953, himself creating its electronically generated tones and tonal qualities (pitch, volume, duration) in strictly rational patterns. This 'musical homunculus' opened up the possibility of a world of all conceivable tones and noises. This absolute control of acoustic tone was diametrically opposed to the Zen Buddhist gesture of complete relinquishment, which John Cage created in his silent piece, *4′ 33″*. The time structure of the work's three movements was determined with the aid of the Chinese I Ching oracle. But the 'composer' here makes no indication of notes since the music consists of any accidental noises that can be heard during these 4 minutes and 33 seconds.

This raises questions, such as: What *is* music? Is anything we hear music? Is everything my ear receives already music? And finally: Where do we stand as human beings in all these matters? In recent decades there has been a great deal of research to show that this art form, specifically, has a profound effect on the human being.[3]

In the birth pangs of these new developments, Rudolf Steiner's reflections on the 'world of music', as this compilation shows, can offer us new perspectives and reveal deeper strata of experience. The quotation above—'The true nature of music, the spiritual element in music, is found between the tones, lies in the intervals as an inaudible quality' – may seem too intangible for some. Rudolf Steiner regards the essence of music as something spiritual, inaudible to the senses; and the world of tones, borne on the vibrations of air, in some sense already as a kind of 'banishment' from this loftier condition.[4]

Thus the seven chapters of this collection of texts start with the intrinsic world of music as Rudolf Steiner sees it: the realm of the spiritually resonating harmonies of the spheres. It is here that we dwell during sleep and in the period between death and rebirth. The astonishing potencies of this music of the spheres appear, for instance, in the chemistry of earthly substances or in the growth and developing morphology of plants.

Chapter 2 identifies how this music of the spheres is connected with humans, our inner and outer form being the outcome of this world, as Rudolf Steiner describes in many diverse ways. Following this, we explore the art of music itself in relation to this realm: the creative shaping of tones by human beings. The works of great composers can give expression to memories or echoes of these harmonies of the spheres. From 1915, Rudolf Steiner offered stimulus for a new kind of composition drawn from a deepened experience of the single tone. Independently of Steiner, various composers since then have been preoccupied with the phenomenon of the individual tone—for instance, the Italian Giancinto Scelsi, French composers of the 'Spectral' school such as Gérard Grisey and Tristan Murail, joined more recently by Wolfgang von Schweinitz. These compositions and experiments are largely concerned with the acoustic spectrum of a tone, whereas Steiner was engaging with the spiritual, moral realm of tone experience.[5]

For Rudolf Steiner, the essence of music consists of the intervals and their qualities, as chapter 4 reveals. These qualities are the inwardly sensed movements between tones. Besides this, the intervals also have their significance as, if you like, a musical embodiment of human evolution: from the interval of the ninth in Lemuria through the seventh in Atlantis to the third since the beginning of the modern era. Thus they express the distinctive soul moods inherent in the development of human consciousness.[6]

In chapter 5 the phenomenon of musical listening and experience is accorded its own section. Connecting acoustic with soul-spiritual experience, this theme was one that preoccupied Steiner throughout his life. In 1917, after 30 years of study, he first formulated his findings in this realm in the book *Riddles of the Soul* (GA 21), pointing there to the connection between musical experience and the human being's rhythmic system, especially as this works in the relationship between cerebrospinal fluid and breathing. Since then, findings in modern neurological research have confirmed his discoveries.[7]

Chapter 6 concerns the view of music of both Goethe and Schopenhauer, figures with whom Steiner engaged in his years in Vienna and Weimar, and to whom he repeatedly referred subsequently in his lectures on music. Goethe's phenomenological approach to music seemed significant to Steiner since he felt that it was moving towards a 'spiritual-scientific, anthroposophic approach'.[8] In Schopenhauer's major work, *The World as Will and Idea*, Steiner greatly valued this philosopher's clear and apt account of the art of music and his sense that unconscious human will was at work here, coming to expression in the musical tone itself.

Finally, music played an important part in Rudolf Steiner's own life. He loved music, attended a great many concerts and operas and followed debates in the music world in those years with keen attention. Of the composers of his time he engaged very fully with Richard Wagner and his works. He knew various composers of his generation personally, or witnessed them in the concert hall—figures such as Richard Strauss, Hugo Wolf and Gustav Mahler. He particularly valued Josef Matthias Hauer's reflections on music. Because the latter's views were founded not on acoustics as such but on the spiritual nature of music—the melos—they are a world away from the twelve-tone ideas of Arnold Schoenberg.

1. 'MUSICA MUNDANA'—THE MUSIC OF THE SPHERES AS UNIVERSAL FORCE

The music of the spheres as a structural cosmic principle was taught from ancient times in the great cultures of China and Egypt, and in particular at the school of Pythagoras in Greece and in Plato's philosophy. Subsequently, the teachings on music in De institutione musicae *by the Neoplatonist Boethius (*c. AD *480 to 524) described music in terms of a threefold 'musica mundana', 'musica humana' and 'musica instrumentalis';*[9] *and this view held sway well into the late medieval period. Rudolf Steiner did not offer a comprehensive account of the music of the spheres and its actions upon the earth but, drawing upon his own research, did identify certain aspects of this, some of which are reproduced from his lectures and writings in the passage below. In his basic text,* Theosophy *(GA 9), Rudolf Steiner gives a general introduction to this world of purely spiritual musical resonance, which the sensory ear cannot perceive. For the 'seer' who has undergone esoteric schooling, it becomes spiritually perceptible as a second realm of spiritual discernment: spiritual vision of the 'archetypes' is joined by spiritual hearing of the 'primal tones'. This world of archetypes and primal tones is in continual movement and ceaseless creative activity.*

In the world of spirit everything is in continual activity and movement, in ceaseless creation. There is no such thing there as resting in one place, as we know it in the physical world. The archetypes are *creating beings*. They are the creators who craft everything that arises in the physical and soul world.

Their forms swiftly change; and in every archetype lies the potential to assume countless different forms. In a sense they allow the specific forms to emerge from them, and no sooner is one engendered than the archetype begins to bring forth another. And the archetypes all have a greater or lesser affinity with each other: they do not act in isolation. Each needs the help of the other to be creatively active. Countless different archetypes frequently work together in order for one or another entity to arise in the physical or soul world.

Apart from what can be perceived through spiritual vision in this 'spirit land', there is something else as well that can be regarded as an experience of 'clairaudience' or spiritual hearing. The moment the seer rises into the land of soul and spirit, the archetypes he perceives also become spiritually *audible* as music. This 'music' is still a purely spiritual process and must be conceived as being devoid of any physical tone. The observer feels himself to be within an ocean of tones; and in these tones, in this spiritual music, the beings of the world of spirit come to utterance and expression. These melodious accords, their harmonies, rhythms and melodies, express the primordial laws of existence. What our reason perceives as law or idea in the physical world becomes apparent to the 'spiritual ear' as a spiritual-musical element. (This is why the Pythagoreans called these perceptions of the spiritual world a 'music of the spheres'. To someone who has developed a 'spiritual ear', this 'music of the spheres' is not merely metaphorical or allegorical but a spiritual reality with which he is fully conversant.) If one wishes to form a proper idea of this 'spiritual music', though, one first has to relinquish all ideas drawn from audible music as perceived by the 'material ear'. These perceptions are spiritual in nature, and thus inaccessible to the sensory ear. [...] We need only conceive of everything that is described as luminous in a visual sense as being, at the same time, also musical in nature. Every colour, every light perception, corresponds to a spiritual tone; and every interplay of colours corresponds to a harmony, a melody and so forth. We must realize that the presence of tones does not mean that 'visual' spiritual perceptions cease; the 'sounds' join the 'light' perceptions. Thus wherever we speak of the spiritual 'archetypes' we must also conceive of them accompanied by spiritual 'tones'.[10]

In the following passage, Steiner illustrates the mathematical and astronomical relationships underpinning the harmonies of the spheres.

Let us now consider the nature of the music of the spheres. I am well aware that modern mathematical astronomers would regard it as pure madness to speak of the planets as esoteric science does. Nevertheless these things are true.

We have spoken of the gradual evolution of our earth and of diverse embodiments of this planet. Our earth was originally Saturn, then became Sun and Moon and is now Earth.* In future times it will become Jupiter, Venus and then Vulcan. Now you may ask this: Today we see a planet Saturn in the heavens; does this have a connection with the Saturn by which we call our planet's first embodiment? Observing the starry heavens we see the planets known to us by outward perception. But the names they have been given are not random or arbitrary, as is often the case nowadays—things named after a particular person or inventor. The names are

* Translator's note: initial capitals show the evolutionary stages of our planet as opposed to the planetary bodies (earth, sun, moon) to which the same names are applied.

significant, and were drawn from profound knowledge of the nature of the stars and planets. Since this is no longer practised, the name of Uranus does not have the same deep meaning, for it was discovered at a later date. The planet you now see in the heavens as Saturn is currently at the stage of evolution that our earth was at when in its 'Saturn' condition. The exoteric Saturn is related to our earth in the same way that a young boy relates to an old man. Just as little as the old man has grown from the boy standing beside him—though he himself was once a boy—so likewise the earth did not evolve from what we now call Saturn. The Saturn we see in the heavens will also one day become 'Earth'; at present its condition is much younger. And the same is true of the other planetary bodies. The sun is an entity such as the earth once was, but is now more 'advanced'. And just as various ages of human beings exist side by side, boys next to old men, so the various planets coexist in the heavens at diverse evolutionary stages which our earth, currently in its fourth embodiment, has in part already passed through and in part will still undergo. The planets have quite specific relationships with each other, but the esotericist expresses these relationships in ways that are different from a modern astronomer.

As you know, the planets orbit the sun at quite specific speeds. But the sun also moves, and it is this movement, as well as that of the planets, which esoteric investigators have carefully determined. This research has shown that the sun circles round a spiritual centre, and that the paths of the planets are spirals oriented to the sun's ecliptic. The speeds at which the various planets accomplish their orbits have very precise, harmonious relationships, which for the clairaudient together form a symphony referred to by the Pythagoreans as the music of the spheres. This harmony, this music, is thus a reflection of cosmic processes; and what the Pythagorean school teaches is not something artificially constructed. Ancient astronomers said that the heavens, which appear to be at rest, are in reality in movement, and that the speed of their orbit around the spiritual centre means that they advance by one degree in every hundred years. The different respective speeds of the planets are as follows:

Speed of Saturn = 2½ times that of Jupiter
of Jupiter = 5 times that of Mars
of Mars = twice that of the sun, Mercury and Venus
of the sun = 12 times that of the moon.

The speed of Saturn is therefore 1200 times greater than that of the whole heavens, thus advancing 12 degrees a year.

When physical, musical harmonies arise, this is because, for instance, different strings vibrate at different speeds. Depending on the rapidity of the strings' vibrations, a higher or lower tone resounds; and the interplay or concord of these different tones sounds forth as music, gives rise to harmony. Now just as you gain musical impressions here in the physical realm from the movements of the strings, so someone who has risen to the level of clairaudience in Devachan will hear the music of the spheres. And through the relationship of the different speeds at which the planets move, the basic tones of the harmonies of the spheres arise and resound through the whole cosmos. In the school of Pythagoras, therefore, people speak quite rightly of a music of the spheres, and one can hear this with spiritual ears.

In these reflections we can point to another phenomenon as well, the 'Chladni' patterns. If you take a thin brass plate and strew a fine dusting of sand on it, then draw a violin bow down its edge, you not only hear a tone but can see the grains of sand form specific patterns and shapes. All kinds of figures arise as expression of different tones. Each one causes substance to be differently distributed.

When spiritual tone first resounded through the cosmos, it ordered and arranged the planets' reciprocal relationships, creating the harmonies of the spheres. What you now see spread across the heavens was given its forms by this creative, divine tone; and by virtue of the fact that this tone sounded forth into cosmic space, matter was ordered and shaped to form the solar system. The expression 'harmony of the spheres' is therefore not just an inventive metaphor but an actual reality.[11]

In 1910, in a brief passage in his lecture cycle on the folk souls in Christiania/Oslo, Steiner again speaks of the music of the spheres, this time from the point of view of the angelic beings who are at work in this realm.

Initially a person has no organs of perception to gaze upwards into what lies beyond the powers of light, which we also call the Spirits of Form; no organs to discern what is interwoven with the light. Everything that determines composition and decomposition on our earth and acts on these processes as chemical forces is here still woven into the light; and this is largely the sphere in which the Spirits of Movement are at work. When a person learns to perceive something of what he otherwise sees only as *maya* in the actions of chemical compositions and dissolutions, then he hears these Spirits of Movement, perceiving the music of the spheres to which the esoteric Pythagoreans, along with other mystery schools, refer. This is also what Goethe describes when he speaks of the sun not as the bestower of light but as a resounding entity:

The sun in ancient guise competing
With brother spheres in rival song,
With thunder march his orb completing
Moves his predestined course along.*

This music of the spheres is still present today, though ordinary consciousness does not discern it. It is real and exists, and approaches all of us from without as astral action. It is just that people do not hear it. If, as is the case with light, the music of the spheres alternated with periods when it disappeared, then people would learn to hear it at certain times. In fact, it resounds ceaselessly day and night and so we can only hear it when we have undergone a certain esoteric schooling and development. Whereas light streams towards us during the day, and weaves on during the night as the light that has been received and absorbed, the music of the spheres sounds day and night. Thus, like the miller who only hears the sound of the mill when it stops turning, we usually fail to hear it.

There are also the Spirits of Wisdom, who send their impulses to us from without, working in to the weaving light and the music of the spheres that weaves through space. Their emanation is the cosmic ether that streams towards the earth. Life streams from the cosmos down to earth and is received and assimilated by the beings there. This comes from the Spirits of Wisdom.

Thus we raise our gaze to far distances of the cosmos and initially look towards the sun in which we see these powers concentrated, and can recognize how the threefold qualities of the second hierarchy, of *streaming life, weaving tone and configuring light,* enter the earthly sphere from space.[12]

---

*Translated by Anna Swanwick, 1909.

During the night our soul dwells in the world of the music of the spheres; but in the day, though it still sounds forth, we cannot experience it until we undergo esoteric schooling.

Now something else occurs by virtue of the fact that the rational or mind soul lifts each night into the astral world. If we use this spiritual-scientific term 'rational soul', we must conceive of it as different from the dry, prosaic rationality that this word usually evokes for us. For spiritual science, 'mind' or 'reason' means a sense of the harmony that cannot be embodied in outward substance or matter, a sense for the inner experience of harmony. This is why we also use the word 'sensibility' here.* Each night the mind soul or 'sensibility soul' immerses itself in the harmonies of the astral world, and each morning it becomes aware of this again in the astral body—the same astral body that has now returned but which, in modern human beings, is not aware of its inwardness during the night. Each night the following occurs. The mind or sensibility soul lives in what we have always referred to as the music of the spheres, the inner lawfulness of the world of spirit, the harmonies of the spheres of which the ancient school of Pythagoras spoke, meaning conditions in the greater world of spirit that can be heard by someone who raises himself to perceptions of this world. Goethe also referred to this [...] in Part 2 of *Faust*, when Faust is once again raised into the spiritual world and says:

> Spirit ears now hear sound forth
> The day once more in its rebirth;
> Hear rocky gates' great opening clang

---

*Translator's note: *Gemuet*, which strongly suggests a feeling, sensitive mind.

And Phoebus' chariot wheels ring.
What a racket does light bring!
Thunderous it trumpets, blares
To blinking eyes, astonished ears . . .

In other words, during the night the soul lives in these sounds of the spheres, which are kindled to awareness as the astral body becomes conscious again.[13]

When we awaken in the morning, returning to our body from the world of the music of the spheres, we can often discern an echo of this world.

Some of you may have noticed that if you attend a concert in the evening which makes a vivid impression on you, when you wake up the next morning you feel as if your soul were lifting itself out of an ongoing re-experience of the music you heard. It seems as if the soul has listened to the whole concert all over again while you were asleep. But the process involved is more complex than it appears to ordinary awareness. In fact, you see, the soul lifts into consciousness again from impressions of the cosmic music that individualizes itself in the human etheric body. As we return to our etheric body on awakening, the physical body's receptivity to impressions means that everything of the nature of this etheric body is drowned out; but at this moment the human soul translates the individualized cosmic music into the earthly tones we last heard. We can say that these are the 'clothes' that this cosmic music puts on at the moment of awakening since it has a certain affinity with the flood of tones we heard in the concert. Because people are unable in their ordinary awareness to hear this cosmic music, it dresses itself in what is most comparable to it in earthly life—the tones we heard in the concert the evening before. This is what actually underlies an experience that most of you, perhaps, have had.[14]

In the lecture which Steiner gave on 3 November 1912 in Vienna, entitled 'The Latest Findings of Esoteric Research into the Life between Death and Rebirth', he describes the differentiated world of the harmonies of the spheres that extends from this side of the sun through the spheres of Mars, Jupiter to Saturn.

We then arrive in the Mars sphere. As long as we were below the sun, we looked outwards towards it. Now the sun is below us and we gaze out into the great expanses of the cosmos. We experience these breadths of space by virtue of what is always called the music of the spheres, though this is little understood—a kind of spiritual music. From then on the visions in which we are immersed have ever less significance while what we hear spiritually assumes more and more importance. The planetary bodies do not appear to us as they do to astronomers on earth, measured and distinguished according to their velocities, but their faster or slower motion instead gives rise to the tones of cosmic harmony. And what we experience inwardly here is an increasing sense that we can only take with us into this region what we spiritually assimilated on earth. By this means we develop our acquaintance with the beings of this sphere, and remain a companionable spirit. Those who shut themselves off from spiritual concerns today, despite their morality or engagement with religious life, cannot enter the spiritual world. There is nothing to be done about it. It is of course fully possible that they will come to this in their next incarnation. All people with a materialistic outlook become hermits when they come to the region beyond the sun, extending to the Mars sphere. However crazy this may sound to some, it is the truth. [...]

In the period I am speaking of, a person lives spiritually in the Mars sphere; then he continues into the Jupiter sphere, where his connection with the earth, which he still retained to a very small degree, now becomes of no significance whatever for him. The sun still exerts a weak effect on him but the wide cosmos, by contrast, acts very powerfully on him. This is what happens: everything acts upon him from without and he absorbs cosmic qualities. The whole cosmos, you see, acts through the harmony of the spheres, which continually assumes different forms the further we explore the life between death and rebirth. This life is hard to describe—these changing harmonies of the spheres. Since one cannot express such things in earthly words, we can use a comparison. The music of the spheres changes as we pass from Mars to Jupiter rather as we experience a transition from orchestral to choral music. Increasingly it becomes tone: the significant quality that at the same time imbues tone, that expresses its living being. The music of the spheres gains content when we enter the sphere of Jupiter, and becomes full content in the sphere of Saturn, an expression of the cosmic Word that created all things, and to which the Gospel of St John refers: 'In the beginning was the Word . . .' This Word is the resounding of cosmic lawfulness and wisdom.[15]

The following introductory words to a eurythmy performance complement the above account. Here he speaks of the spheres of Mars, Jupiter and Saturn without referring to them by name, characterizing their different qualities in relation to the arts of speech and music.

Thus we really return to the principles of ancient temple dancing, since all such temple art was originally founded on the principle of permeating human life with the power of the

Word. This did not mean the word as we usually understand it, but instead the wisdom resounding through the cosmos in the music of the spheres and coming to expression in the most varied realms: a pure reflection in human language, a somewhat more abstract expression in human song, and a materialization of it in instrumental music. This can be redeemed if, in the way I have described, the whole human organism is brought into dynamic configuration and movement.[16]

Now follow three lecture passages from the year 1908, which depict the tangible effects of the harmonies of the spheres upon our earth, its physical substances and the growth and form of plants.

And now we come once more to an important matter. Just as light was created at the same time as air, so, as air condensed into water, something similar arose. In the same way that air and light are related, water relates to sound, tone. Tone can of course pass through air, and initiates vibrations there, thus becoming audible. Yet tone as such emerged on earth alongside the creation of water. And just as light effects stream through the air, so all the water to which air condensed—the earth now of course consisting of heat, air and water—bore tone vibrating everywhere through it. In the regions where our earth became most watery it was also most pervaded by all possible tonal harmonies streaming into it; and the result of these actions of tone in the water is something very, very important. Naturally you have to imagine that these ancient, primal waters, these waters of the earth, contained all the substances that were later deposited as metals, minerals and so on. It is really especially interesting to turn our inner gaze to these ancient times and to see how the most diverse forms emerge from fluid through the form-creating tone at work in water. Tone creates forms and shapes in water. This was a really wonderful period of our earth's evolution. On a large scale what happened then resembles what occurs if you strew fine sand on a metal plate and then stroke it with a violin bow. The Chladni patterns appear, very regular patterns as you know. Thus, through the music streaming from cosmic space, the most varied forms and figures appeared; and the substances that were dissolved in the fluid hearkened to this cosmic music and were shaped and ordered accordingly. This dance of substances to the tune of cosmic music gave rise, most importantly, to protein, to protoplasm, as the foundation of all life. However much materialists ponder the mechanical actions that they think gave rise to protein from oxygen, nitrogen, carbon and so on, in fact it formed from cosmic matter through the harmonies of cosmic music. Living substances are patterned in accordance with this cosmic music. Around and especially within the subtle structures I spoke of there formed the proteinous substance, the protoplasm, that pervades everything. Lengthwise along the lines I described to you as lines of heat or warmth runs the fluid that has coagulated to protein through the action of cosmic tone, and this gradually passes into blood formation. In the nerve lines this coagulated fluid forms protein. And the protein first developed as a kind of envelope, a cartilaginous calcium substance you might say, to form a protection against the outside world. All this did really develop in accordance with the dance of substances as governed by the music of the spheres.[17]

Now the time came when the sun emerged from the earth again, or crystallized from it. The finest substances and beings formed an autonomous heavenly body so that our earth began to orbit the sun. With the emergence of the finest materials a densification of the remaining matter occurred. On the one hand the fine, luminous sun body emerged and, on the other, the matter of the earth became much denser and entered into a fluid condition, but denser than our ocean water is today, since it contained everything that is now solid. As water or fluid develops, a new element appears. The music of the spheres, the cosmic tones, pervade the earth to the degree that water appears there. This was not music as we know it now, which is conveyed through the air. The evolution of the earth was governed by this cosmic music. Separate substances solidified from the great undifferentiated breadth of matter, beginning to dance under the influence of this cosmic music. Matter diversified into all the organic substances, for instance protein. Thus organic matter, protoplasm arose under the influence of cosmic music, similar to the way the Chladni patterns appear today.[18]

When, in esoteric development, you rise to a plant consciousness permeated by the bright day consciousness of your I, then you reach the level of Inspiration, of inspired consciousness. This inspired consciousness does not only work pictorially. When what flows from things enters another being, this consciousness cannot be compared with picture consciousness but is a sounding, resounding one. Here we enter a spiritual world of tones; it is a form of consciousness which Pythagoras referred to as the harmony of the spheres. The whole world expresses its nature through tone; and when we fall asleep at night, when our astral body departs with the I from our physical and etheric body, the harmonies and melodies of cosmic music penetrate this astral body, and it is then embedded in its own true spiritual existence, acquiring from the music of the spheres the capacity to replace the powers that have been exhausted. During the night we plunge down into the music of the spheres, and because its tones resound through us, we feel renewed and strengthened in the morning. When we become aware of this we are in Inspiration consciousness and are able to perceive all that exists within our solar system. Whereas our ordinary thinking capacity grasps only earthly things, Imagination enables us to enter into correspondence with the beings of the various planets, and into connection with the whole solar system when we attain Inspiration. In certain circles people have always known this. Goethe, who was an unconscious initiate, knew it. And this is why, in the Prologue of *Faust*, which takes place in heaven, the world of spirit, the angels say these words:

> The sun in ancient guise competing
> With brother spheres in rival song...

We see here that he knows that all mysteries of the solar system come to expression in tones, and that someone who raises himself to the level of Inspiration can learn of these mysteries. That Goethe does not write this arbitrarily can be seen in the fact that he reiterates it in Part 2 of *Faust*, when he raises his protagonist into the world of spirit:

> Spirit ears now hear sound forth
> The day once more in its rebirth...

'Spirit ears' are those of the clairvoyant or clairaudient, who perceives the solar system's harmony of the spheres. And if you were able to actually perceive the solar forces that stream down upon physical plants as they grow from the earth, these plant bodies with their roots and leaves, culminating above in flowering organs where the astral body suffuses them, and into which the spiritual powers of the sun penetrate—if you could perceive these powers entering mysteriously through the blossom, you would hear them as the spiritual music of the spheres, which only the ears of spirit can hear. Spiritual tones everywhere penetrate plant blossoms; and the secret of plant growth is that in every single flower one finds an expression of tones that form it, giving the fruit its distinct character. The plant assimilates the sun's tones, which indwell it as spirit. You may know that one can use tone to create forms in the material world. In the Chladni experiments tone forms are created on a metal plate on which fine sand is strewn—the tone orders and patterns the sand, which gives visual expression to the nature of the tone that has formed it. And just as the physical tone is here in a sense captured by the sand, so flowers and fruit capture and assimilate the sun's spiritual tone. It is hidden in the seed, mysteriously and secretly; and when a new plant grows from it, then the captured, assimilated sun tone is what conjures the form of the plant once more. Clairvoyant consciousness looks upon the plant world surrounding us and sees in the tapestry of flowers covering the earth a reflection of the sun's tones. And so what Goethe says is true: the sun resounds. But it is also true to say that these sun tones stream down and are absorbed by the plants, then reappear again when a new plant emerges from a seed. In the forms of plants the sun's tones reverberate back into space as a reflection of the music of the spheres. And so we see how world and earth, how the fixed stars and the planets, are inwardly connected. We learn not only to see what exists in our physical surroundings but we also gain an inkling of how someone who partakes of Inspiration rises sunwards.[19]

2. THE HUMAN BEING AS MUSIC—'MUSICA HUMANA'

The human being and his various 'bodies'—physical body, etheric body, astral body and I—are configured by the spiritual resonances of the powers of the planets and zodiac, as are our inner organs such as lungs, liver and the nervous system, and our skeletal system. Here Steiner gives an outline of the physical and etheric body as a reflection of the cosmic music of the spheres.

If we succeed through meditation of an appropriate kind in breaking through our memory pictures, in a sense, and discarding what sunders us inwardly from the etheric body and the physical body, and if we then look down into the etheric body and physical body so that we perceive what lies there below the threshold of awareness, then we hear tones in both these bodies. And these tones are the echo of the cosmic music of the spheres which we have assimilated in the life between death and rebirth during our descent from the divine, spiritual world towards the physical world, towards incarnation in what our parents and ancestors give us as physical inheritance. In our etheric body and physical body the music of the spheres continues to resonate: as vowel quality in the etheric body and consonantal quality in the physical body.

It is true to say that as we take our way through life between death and rebirth we make our way upwards, as you will remember, into the world of the higher hierarchies. We have seen how the human being lives his way into the world of the Angeloi, Archangeloi and Archai, how he lives within these angelic hierarchies in a way that resembles how he lives here amongst the entities and creatures of the plant and animal kingdoms. Following this life between death and rebirth, he descends to earthly life again. And we have seen that in this journey he takes with him, initially, the actions of the fixed stars or their zodiac representation, and then, as he descends further, also the influences of the planetary spheres, of the circling planets.

Now let us recall this zodiac, the representation of the fixed stars. The human being is exposed to these influences as he descends from spiritual life into earthly life. The intrinsic nature of these influences is something we can rightly call 'cosmic consonantal music'. Here we have consonants, and this consonantal action in the physical body is the echo of the various musical configurations of the zodiac. The movements of the planets is the vowel quality within this cosmic music of the spheres, and this imbues the etheric body. In our physical body therefore we unconsciously bear a reflection of cosmic consonance, and in our etheric body a reflection of cosmic vowel qualities.

[...] We have said nothing by saying merely that we consist of a physical and etheric body. This is only a vague and obscure generality. To speak in the real language that can be learned from the secrets of the cosmos, we would have to say that we consist of the echo of the fixed stars, the echo of the planetary movements, of what experiences this echo of planetary movements, and of what consciously experiences the echo of the fixed stars. Then we would have expressed in the real language of the cosmos what we only utter in an abstract form by saying that we consist of a physical body, etheric body, astral body and I.[20]

Describing the etheric body here as an echo of the planetary movements, Steiner refers to the astral body in the same context as 'the experience of these planetary movements'. In a lecture on education, he takes up the theme of the astral body again as a particularly musical element.

The astral body expresses itself in the physical body, and the way it does so can be understood according to natural laws. But we cannot understand the astral body itself, its inner nature and action, according to natural laws but only by developing an inner, musical understanding alongside outward comprehension. This kind of insight existed in the Orient, became attenuated in Greek times, and in our modern age has faded entirely. In the same way that the etheric body works out of cosmic sculpting, so the astral body works out of cosmic music, cosmic melodies. The only earthly aspect of the astral body is the musical pulse, whereas the elements of rhythm and melody work entirely out of the cosmos. And the astral body consists of rhythm and melody. What we derive from natural laws will not enable us to approach the astral body but only what we acquire by developing an inner understanding of music. Then we will find, when the interval of a third is played, for instance, that there is something present there which we feel and experience as if inside us. This may be a major or minor third; and in our feeling life, through this structuring of the scale, considerable differences can be elicited. It is still inner experience. When we come to the fifth, this is experienced instead at the surface of our skin—the boundary between us and the outer world. Here we feel as if we are still, just, within ourselves. As we come to the sixth or the seventh, we can sense that these intervals seek to unfold outside us. In the fifth we emerge from ourselves and, arriving at the sixth and seventh, we experience what occurs there as something outside us. The third, by contrast is eminently inward in quality. The astral body is at work here, as a musician inside every person; it imitates the cosmic music. And everything of this kind existing within us in turn comes to active expression in the development of the human form. If we begin to grasp this, it can radically affect the way we understand the world, can shake up all our views.

You see, what passes from the astral body into form, and is not already founded in the cosmic sculpting process but arises instead because musical impulse emanates from the astral body and permeates the human being, is something we can actually study in detail if we can bring a musical understanding to bear on the human form as we previously applied sculptural understanding to study the actions of the etheric body. If you look at the part of the human organism that starts at the shoulder blades and descends from there to the arms, this is an effect of the prime, the ground tone alive in the human being. As we come to the interval of the second we find this located in the upper arm. These things become apparent through eurythmy. Continuing to the lower arm, we have the third, both the major and minor third in music. In reaching this interval of the third, we find two bones in the lower arm. And so it continues right into our fingers. This may sound schematic but it is as true for spiritual-scientific observation as a mathematical deduction is true for a mathematician. This is not something based on obscure mysticism but can be studied in precise detail.[21]

In a lecture which he gave on 29 December 1914, during the early period of building work on the Goetheanum in Dornach, when

Steiner was surrounded by numerous artists, he speaks of the astral body as a 'very complex configuration' and describes its tangible connection with the element of music. These lectures were later published under the title Art as Seen in the Light of Mystery Wisdom *(GA 275).*

Let us now deepen our reflections a little; but as we do so we need to realize that the human organization is really not as simple as people find it convenient to imagine. It is really extremely easy and convenient to picture the human being consisting of physical body, etheric body, astral body, I and so forth. It is easy to be satisfied by merely listing these things and gaining an approximate understanding of them. And yet things are not that simple. These are not vessels that are simply stacked on top of each other—physical body, etheric body, astral body and I; but they are, rather, very complex configurations. And if, for instance, one focuses on the astral body, it is wrong to say that this can be seen as a single thing. The matter is more complex.

The astral body for instance—and here words are fairly inadequate approximations—must be seen as inwardly structured. It consists of seven parts. Just as we ourselves have seven parts—physical body, etheric body, astral body, I, Spirit Self, Life Spirit, Spirit Man—so the astral body likewise permeates all these aspects. We can say that the 'thinnest' part of the astral body has been primarily formed and adapted to the physical body. The astral body is organized according to different laws in each of our constituent aspects—in the physical body, the etheric body, within itself, in the I, in the Spirit Self, in the Life Spirit, and in Spirit Man. In each it comes to expression differently. Each of these aspects is sevenfold in turn; and so, when we consider this sevenfold human nature, and realize that each is also sevenfold, we can see that 49 aspects exist. Naturally this is a ghastly thought for modern psychology, which prefers to see the soul as a single unity, and does not wish to contemplate such complexity. But for real insight, increasingly necessary as humanity evolves, this is not without importance. If we know that the astral body is sevenfold in nature, and that it is an organism of living inner impulses, we can recognize that processes are also occurring between the diverse aspects of this sevenfold astral body. The part of the astral body that corresponds to the physical body has a certain reciprocal relationship with the part of the astral body corresponding to the etheric body, and likewise with the part that corresponds to the astral body itself, and so forth. And these are not merely abstract assumptions. For instance, in the human organism it can certainly happen that we inwardly sense—though more subconsciously than consciously—a stirring in the part of the astral body that corresponds to the physical body. And then some factor or other can cause a further stirring that necessarily begins in the part of the astral body that corresponds to the astral body itself, and so on. But this actually happens—it is not mere theory.

Picture this: the seven aspects of the astral body are in the same reciprocal relationship as the tones of the scale—prime, second, third, fourth and so on. When you give yourself up to the effect of a melody, the nature of your human organization is such that any tone within a melody will be experienced in the corresponding part of the astral body. A third is experienced in the part of the astral body that corresponds to the astral body itself. A fourth is experienced in the part of the astral body which—well, let's describe this in more detail—corresponds to the mind or sensibility soul. A fifth is experienced in the part of the astral body corresponding to the consciousness soul. And if you recall that a more careful division of things gives us nine parts, we must divide the astral body accordingly. I could list this all as follows, in the way we are now considering it: the part of the astral body corresponding to the physical body is experienced in the prime, the ground tone; the part of the astral body corresponding to the etheric body is experienced in the second; the part corresponding to the astral body itself is experienced in the third.

	—	
	—	
	—	
Fifth	—	consciousness soul
Fourth	—	mind soul
Third	—	astral body (sentient soul/astral body)
Second	—	etheric body
Prime	—	physical body

But now you can also see that the presence of the major third and the minor third really does correspond to the way the astral body is embedded in and integrated into our whole human organization. Look at the relevant section in my book *Theosophy*. We have a concordance on the one hand with what we call the astral body and, on the other, with what we call the sentient soul. And thus what I referred to as the third can correspond to the astral body *or* the sentient soul: the major third in the first instance, the minor third in the second.

Our response to a piece of music does actually depend on this inner musical activity of the astral body. We listen to the music with our I but then immediately plunge this experience down into our astral body, into certain subconscious regions.

But this leads us to a very important thing. Let us consider ourselves in so far as we are an astral being, or bear an astral being within us. What is this nature of ours? We have been created out of the cosmos as astral being according to musical laws. As an astral being, we have a musical connection with the cosmos. We ourselves are an instrument.

Now let us assume that we did not need tones to be physically audible but that we could listen to the creative activity in the cosmos which created us, our astral organization, then we would hear the cosmic music that has always been called the music of the spheres. Let us assume we were able to plunge consciously into our astral being and could elevate this astral being to such potency, such spiritual potency, that we heard the creative activities of the cosmic music. If this were so we could say that the cosmos was playing our own being, with the aid of our astral body. This thought as I express it now was very much alive in people in ancient times. This in turn can show us the whole process of materialization of human evolution that occurred as the fifth post-Atlantean era advanced, for this idea no longer lives in humanity's modern exoteric culture. Humanity no longer has any sense that we are musical instruments as far as our astral bodies are concerned. But this was not always true, and we have, if you like, forgotten this. There was a time when people recalled the figure of John, one who was able to put himself in a spiritual condition so that he could hear the music of the heavenly Jerusalem. They saw that all earthly music can only be a reflection or echo of this heavenly music that began with the creation of the human being. And those of more religious sensibility felt that by embracing the desires of the physical world the human being assimilated impulses that obscure and dissipate the heavenly music. At the same time, though, they felt it was necessary to pursue a path in human evolution through purification of external, chaotic life that would lead, in a sense, to listening through outward, material music to the spiritual music of the cosmos again.

This relationship between outer, material music with its divine origins, its archetype as heavenly music in the world of spirit, was beautifully expressed in the tenth and eleventh centuries in the prompting to make music a kind of religious service or act of worship, to become aware that in engendering tones people should free themselves from their constriction in a merely chaotic and, as they felt it to be, impure outer world. People felt the life of ordinary, outward language to be impure. They felt elevated to spiritual heights when they raised themselves from such speech to their musical reflection of heavenly music. This was expressed in the following words: '*Ut* queant laxis *re*sonare fibris *mi*ra gestorum *fa*muli tuorum *so*lve polluti *la*bii reatum, *S.J.*—Sancte Johanne.'

This can be translated as: 'So that your servants may sing the wonders of your works with resonant vocal cords, cleanse now the sins of lips grown earthly (in other words lips that have become capable of speech), Saint John.' You see, the one who could hear the heavenly Jerusalem was the figure to whom people looked up in this context. And you get the whole scale here by taking the *ut*, which later became 'do', the re from *resonare*, the mi from *mira*, the fa from *famuli*, the sol from *solve*, the la from *labii*; and *S.J.* is si, or 'ti'. This produced the solfa, used as notation in medieval times: this is hidden in this verse.

Through atavistic clairvoyance this knowledge lived into the eleventh and twelfth centuries but began to fade as the materialistic world-view grew dominant. Such knowledge ebbed from human awareness. Now, though, we live in a time when, through spiritual cognition, we must find our way back to this, must recreate it. Everything can show us that evolution descended so deeply that humankind found itself in a kind of swamp. The murky waters of this swamp are all the materialistic ideas that developed. But now we are slowly working our way out of this materialistic swamp again, are ascending again, and must rediscover what humanity lost as it descended.

Yesterday I suggested that we do not only sleep at night but that something in us is also asleep in the daytime. At night the thinking-feeling element is more asleep whereas during the day the will-feeling element tends to sleep. When we allow the I to immerse itself in the astral body, we descend into this element of feeling and will. When a work of music resounds what happens is that our I nature consciously descends into the otherwise sleeping element. If you are sitting there listening to a symphony, this involves an inner process whereby your ordinary, mundane thinking life is dulled and you immerse your soul-spiritual apprehension in something that is otherwise asleep during waking life. Thus music connects us with all the enlivening powers in the human organism, with all that in a sense pervades and invigorates us, allowing us to become one, if you like, with streaming currents of tone.

At night we sleep. Here mundane thinking is dulled in an element that we do not possess in our ordinary awareness. But when we succeed in bringing back into our ordinary waking consciousness what is awoken in the sleeping human being, the element we live in during sleep is immersed in waking life. Please note the contradiction I have just uttered. I first said that our I experience, when we listen to music, is submerged in what sleeps in us during the day, and now I am saying that we immerse what we experience during the night in our waking consciousness. When this happens it becomes poetry. People such as Plato felt this to be true when they called poetry a divine dreaming.

The arts can teach us to reflect on our connection with the whole cosmos in a vivid way rather than just as schematic concepts. Please be aware that these things are not merely schematic in nature. Some people feel very pleased when they can neatly order and categorize things such as those presented in my book *Theosophy*. And I'm sure that some people regard it as wayward of me to present the three interconnecting triads in a way that deviates from what they previously learned in an anthroposophic context. But if one engages with actual experience, the reality of the matter, we can see that major and minor modes are deeply rooted by their very nature in the whole structure of the cosmos. Only when we draw on the whole, living structure of the cosmos do these things correspond to reality.[22]

The astral body is physically elaborated in the nervous system. The ancient Greeks referred to this as the 'lyre of Apollo'.

You have to inwardly hear the human being's astral body. It is the 'third man' in us, the one we comprehend when we advance to empty consciousness, and allow this emptiness to be filled by inspirations we receive.

Language itself is really cleverer than human beings themselves, for it originates in primordial times. There are profound reasons why breathing was called 'inspiration'. In general the words of our language have far more to tell us than we usually recognize with our abstract consciousness.

These are things that can lead us initially to the three

aspects of human nature: the physical body, etheric body, and astral body, expressed in our air, fluid and solid organisms. They have their physical counterparts in the solid physical structures of our body, in the fluctuating and transforming configurations of our system of fluids, and in what pervades us as an inner music experienced in our feeling life. The nervous system is the loveliest reflection of this inward music, and is constructed out of the astral body, out of inward music. This is why at one place this nervous system has the wonderful form of the spinal cord to which the various nerve strands attach. All this together forms a wonderful musical fabric that is continually at work in us, working up into the head.

A primordial wisdom that still lived in ancient Greece recognized this wonderful instrument within us, coming into effect as the air we breathe in rises up through the whole spinal cord. The air we breathe in enters the spinal cord and rises towards the brain. This music really is performed though we remain unaware of it. All that reaches our awareness is the repercussion of it. Here we have the lyre of Apollo, this interior musical instrument that was still recognized by primordial wisdom.[23]

As the 'lyre of Apollo' the human being is like a musical instrument, and in fact the 'most perfect in the whole world'.

When we study the secrets of music we discover, as I said on a previous occasion here, what the Greeks meant when they spoke with such insight of the lyre of Apollo. Our musical experience involves an intrinsically human adaptation to the inner harmonies and melodies of cosmic existence from which we originate, which have shaped and formed us. The nerves which emerge from our spinal cord are really wonderful strings whose function has undergone a metamorphosis. This is the lyre of Apollo, this spinal cord, ending above in the brain, with its separate nerve strands extending throughout the body. Upon these nerve strands the soul and spirit is played within the earthly world. We ourselves are the most perfect instrument in the world; and an external musical instrument conjures tones for us as artistic experience in so far as we feel in its resonating strings, say, something that is connected with our own constitution of nerves and blood vessels, with our bodily structure. Our neurosensory system is inwardly configured music, and we experience music as an artistic quality to the degree that a piece of music is in tune with the mystery of our own musical structure.[24]

If we ask why many works of music so deeply move us, we must remember that our inner being as microcosm, configured by the music of the cosmos, here experiences a resonance with the macrocosm.

We can learn to perceive resounding tone as dual in nature: firstly in its 'banishment' in the air, conveyed with the latter's vibrations, or also in its own intrinsic realm in the world of imaginations. If we learn to discern it in its own spiritual region, then we see at the same time how the human organization with its internal organs is spiritually configured out of this resonant element, this element of cosmic harmonies and melodies; and then we gain a sense of the inmost nature of the human organization. We learn to recognize that our organs, our lungs and so forth, developed from the choirs of the cosmos, that our whole organism is an outcome of the cosmic music; and then we understand why great works of music so deeply and inwardly move us, why many associate the art of music directly with our interior life whereas they think of the other arts in connection with more outward apprehension.[25]

In the next passage, Rudolf Steiner digresses on the liver, which he describes as being connected in a specific way with music and in particular with the musician.

In clinical practice, in anatomy, a liver is just a liver, whether it is the liver of a 50-year-old, a 25-year-old or that of a musician. The liver of someone who knows as little of music as a cow about Sunday—which eats grass every day of the week whatever day it is—is in fact very different from a musician's liver. And this is because the liver has a great deal to do with the resonance in us of musical ideas. There is no value in ascetically regarding the liver as seemingly unimportant. This liver, seemingly a small organ, is the seat of all that lives in a harmonious sequence of melodies, and it has a great deal to do with listening to a symphony. However, we must be clear that this liver has a corresponding etheric organ and that it is *this* which is primarily connected with musical experience. But the outer physical liver is in fact in a sense the exudate of the etheric liver, and is shaped and configured in the same way.[26]

In the 'Tone Eurythmy Course' (GA 278) Rudolf Steiner gives a striking example of the outward embodiment in us of the musical element: the skeletal structure of our upper movement organism is formed entirely from the seven intervals extending from prime to seventh.

I have often emphasized that eurythmy is drawn from the very nature of the human organization, from the movement potentials prefigured in it. The human organism embodies the musical element as predisposition on the one hand, and on the other—this is particularly relevant to tone eurythmy—music translated into movement. It will be quite evident to you that the musical element has its intrinsic seat more or less in the human breast or just above it. Let us ask where we can find the transition in the human organism itself from singing, from our inner musical organization, to what is available to us in the movement organism of eurythmy. To discern this—and this is immediately obvious—we must look at the moving parts connected to the chest or breast organism, the limbs which emerge from it.

The arms and hands really are the most wonderful of our human organs. You need only call on what I will call your intuitive apprehension a little to perceive that the elements of our singing organism, the palate, jaws and so forth, are in a sense hardened arms and hands that have come to rest. If you clasp your hands so that the fingers are interlaced and then try to move them about, and then compare this with the way your upper and lower jaw work together—as you can observe in a skeleton—you can easily see, if you add the muscles in your imagination, how something mobile comes to rest.

Now we can see that what serves music in the activity of singing is extended in a downward direction. Surrounded by muscles and bones, though, which end in the arms and hands, we can also see something intrinsically connected with the voice and also with vocal expression. Since making movements depends on using one's muscles and bones, we will need to learn to feel how we must use muscles and bones to perform musical eurythmy.

In singing we ask about voice 'production', with all the aspects belonging to it. Can we therefore also ask about the preconditions necessary for doing eurythmy with our most expressive organs, the arms and hands?

We have a remarkable organ which in a sense provides the anatomical and physiological connection between the trunk and the arm, and this is the clavicle or collarbone. It is shaped like an S. The clavicle is really a wonderful bone. One end of it is connected with our centre and, after forming its S, the other end extends towards the periphery, towards the directing of arms and hands. Please consider the following. Animals which use their forefeet to climb, such as bats or monkeys, have a very aesthetically formed clavicle, whereas those such as raptors, cats, lions, which do not climb but which use their forefeet to tear their prey into morsels, have a less well-developed clavicle, though they do still have one. The horse, which does nothing with its front legs except run, has developed no other skills with these legs and cannot make any subtle movements with its forefeet, has no clavicle at all. Now in the clavicle we can feel the preconditions, the impetus for performing musical eurythmy. It lies there. And when you become aware that a power passes into your arms and hands from the clavicle and its ancillary muscles, then you will be able to do tone eurythmy with great vitality. You will find the conditions for it there. It is really a matter of developing a living feeling for one's limbs so that you can use them for the kinds of movement we demonstrated. If you cannot feel your way into this part of the body you won't find the right impetus.

It is therefore necessary above all for you to prepare for doing tone eurythmy by focusing your awareness on the left and right clavicle. When you begin to perform tone eurythmy, when you come on stage, place your awareness there. You should have a sense that the fine movement possibilities you pour into your arms and hands emanate from your clavicle just as the voice emerges from the conditions for vocal production, the place of vocal attack. You need to feel that you are pouring this feeling, which you consciously elicit in the clavicle, first into the socket of the upper arm. And when your legs, as they move, express the tonic or keynote, have a sense too that as you open your arm the power which performs this is passing to the tonic, from high up, from the arm's place of impetus. You should feel as if the whole lower arm, and even the upper arm too, the whole lower arm and hand and fingers, are very light—as if they have no gravity, as if they are not there at all, as if you were using them in a very airy way. But nevertheless feel a strong impetus here, from the place where the movement originates; and then you have held the tonic, the keynote in your arm. And feel the lifting or turning of your upper arm, feel this in connection with the movement that I showed you for the interval of the second. Feel the second itself when you have to hold your hand in a particular way as you do this, as if the strength to hold the hand in this way proceeds from your upper arm, and then you will properly perform the second; then it will *be* a second.

And now, when what in a sense flows from the clavicle passes beyond the upper arm towards the lower arm, as it does so it becomes the interval of the third—becomes a third. But here something very remarkable occurs. To create the third you make the movement required to form it, which I demonstrated in our first session. You use the lower arm for this, with either hand, the left or right, depending on where you are forming the third. If you now allow the feeling that you used in the upper arm to flow on in this way, you can let it flow down through the elbow into the rear part of the lower arm. This can still be done. Passing over the elbow, you arrive at the place of impetus for the third. Then you can ask this: Can I let the feeling flow this way [along the inner arm forward towards the hand]? If you have a healthy sense for this you will know that this can't be done. Up here I can let the feeling flow down to the back of the hand. But it doesn't work if I make it flow down here [inner arm]. And so I have to picture here that something comes to meet me, comes from below. I have to picture that as I reach my hand out somewhere the feeling flows up this way. Thus there are two possibilities. If this is the place of impetus for the upper arm [see drawing] the feeling can flow on here [downwards], and we come from the second to the third. But we can also elaborate the feeling that comes from the opposite direction towards us, entering from the hand [arrow].

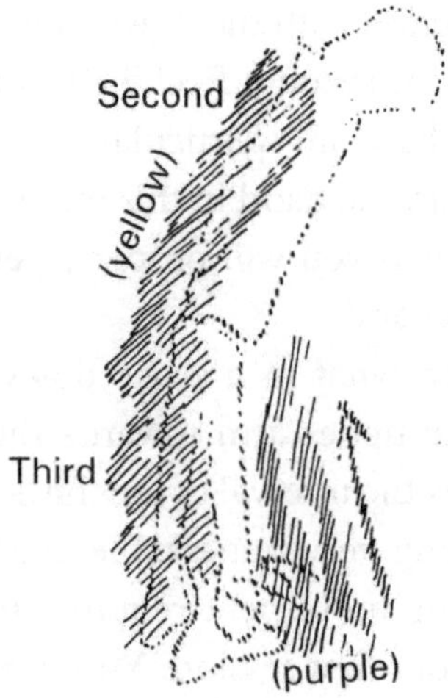

This really is something wonderful! The human arm has an upper arm bone for the second, and two lower arm bones, the ulna and radius, because there are two kinds of third. The rear lower arm bone represents the major third and the front lower arm bone the minor third. The scale lives in the bones and muscles of the arm in a really wonderful way. If you now approach closer to the hand, where the little bones are here, you can still feel very much as if you were still within yourself. We only emerge when we come to the full hand itself. The fourth is still inside us, here at the root of the hand. Here you must feel the movement that gives you the fourth. The fifth is here in the hand itself. The sixth you feel here in the upper fingers, and the seventh, as I showed you, can be done especially with the lower fingers. Here you have to send the feeling right into the lower fingers.

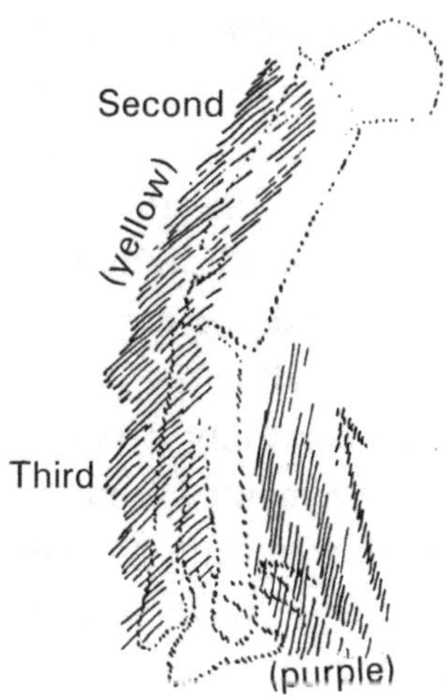

You see, it is not just an empty phrase to say that eurythmy is drawn from the human being's whole organism. It is absolutely drawn from our organism, so much so that we can keep referring to the human skeleton, with the two bones of the lower arm for the major and minor third, so that you must develop here the feeling corresponding to a major and minor scale. You feel the major key in the feeling that flows downwards, over the elbow and into the ulna and then towards the back of the hand. If you feel it flowing towards the back of the hand, you are in the major mode.

But if you feel a small breath of air or a sense of something coming towards you, passing through the palm of the hand and here entering the inner bone of the lower arm, this is the minor feeling. Do try to acquire a sense for such feelings shifting into the human organism, and then you will find that you become very inwardly musical; and then you embody the scale.

It is worth observing two different people doing eurythmy, one of whom forms the movements as if copied externally, formed as if by a mechanical human figure made of papier mâché, and then someone who really feels the impetus in his clavicle, the keynote or tonic at the root of the upper arm, the second starting here [upper arm], the third in the lower arm, and the further intervals, fourth, fifth, sixth and seventh, in the hand itself. In our hands we have to emerge from ourselves, and do so most of all in the lower fingers where the seventh is created. In eurythmy it really isn't a matter of artificially inventing movements but rather of drawing upon the movement potentials that are embodied in the human form, drawing these out of it. In this respect eurythmy is different from all other modern dance forms. If you look at various attempts at new movement arts you will never find that they are drawn in this way from the human being himself. One first has to know that the scale, starting from the clavicle, is embodied in the human arm with the human hand.

It is clear that a horse cannot do eurythmy. This would look awful if it attempted to do so. A cat or kitten doing eurythmy would be a better sight, and a little monkey even better. A small monkey doing eurythmy would probably be a fairly pleasant spectacle. Why? The horse has no clavicle. The cat has a clavicle, although not as well formed as that of a monkey. The more developed the clavicle in an animal, the better you can envisage it doing eurythmy.

Everything arising, emerging from the lungs, larynx and so forth undergoes a corresponding metamorphosis to be outwardly reflected in the connection between the clavicle, shoulder blade (which also has a closing function here), upper arm, lower arm and finger bones.

Now you will certainly have the sense, whenever tones up to the fourth resound or are embodied in eurythmy, that this involves a forward movement. If you sound the scale as far as the fourth—ground note, second, third, fourth—then this is a forward movement. On reaching the fifth you get a sense that something has changed. And with the sixth and seventh you get a clear feeling that an expansion also occurs. The whole scale spreads out. This too is reflected in the structure of the hand. And if you consider the simplicity of the structure of the upper arm and the two bones of the lower arm, this perfectly reflects the first few steps of the scale. Where things expand and spread out you find this embodied in the hand itself, from the interval of the fourth onwards. Here you have 27 bones for inner mobility. You can therefore elaborate a great deal of expressive power specifically in the hand as you come to the higher notes of the scale.

As you know, there are anatomical similarities between the arm and the hand and, though with a less clear place of impetus, the leg and the foot. Although more difficult, it is possible to employ the legs and feet in the kinds of movement you used the arms and hands to convey. Here these movements can only be hinted at really. If you convey the scale through legs and feet, it will be less beautiful but we can try to acquire an expressive quality here, one different from dancing as such, as we have also attempted in diverse ways in speech eurythmy and suchlike. It will become clear for the legs and feet that where the thigh begins, the whole femur, this corresponds to the keynote if you tense its muscles. If you try to move in such a way that the lower leg hangs, in a sense, while the upper leg performs strong, taut movements, you remain in the realm of ground note and second. Passing to the lower leg, to calf and shin, you have the major and minor third again—the major third in the tibia and the minor third in the fibula. Thus you can express the third in the legs too, although there will be a substantial difference here—similar to that between the double bass and the violin—between such movements and our most expressive movements.

Now if you have two people performing together, you can do it like this: the notes down to the tenor c can be strongly articulated with the arm, while lower octaves are made in a corresponding way with the legs, either by the same person or someone else; and you will see there are great expressive possibilities here.

Thus one really can introduce all musical elements into eurythmy. During these lectures it is not possible, of course, for us to do exercises too; but you will understand what I mean. You will need to practise everything we have been speaking of. Practice will bring you fully into its reality. And this, as you will see, will give us the whole tone eurythmy system.[27]

The resounding of the etheric body during the night is caused by the Exusiai.

As we fall asleep we can sense a certain humming and chiming: the flow and rustling of our inner organism. This continues, as we sleep, as a musical activity that is extraordinarily rich in melodies and harmonies and pervades our whole inner reality during sleep. This musical activity lasts from when we fall asleep to when we reawaken. And the I and astral body outside our physical and etheric body are strongly affected by the resounding tones of the etheric body left behind in bed. This shines as well as sounding. But the impression this makes on our I and astral body remains for the time being in the unconscious.

Similarly, etheric currents of warmth stream inwards from the whole surface of our skin. Together with various other aspects that are less discernible than the warmth, light and sound we perceive in the outer world, and which are therefore hard to describe, this all gives rise to a huge and beautiful, majestic, mighty inner stirring, movement and flowing of the human etheric body. It is as if this special resonance and luminosity and streaming flow, the currents of warmth of the individual human etheric body, were rising from the universe like islands from the general etheric sea of the cosmos, doing so for inner reasons which are in fact none other than those at work in the human being himself, his inherent existence. And this warming flow, this phosphorescent luminosity, this musical resonance are also what detach themselves from our astral body and I a few days after death, and stream, flow out into the general universal ether of the cosmos. [...]

You can see, therefore, what complexity there is in the human etheric body. And if we try to penetrate further into such worlds by means that allow us to do so, we find that this warming flow, this phosphorescent luminosity, this flux of music, is the outward revelation of cosmic beings. Everything I have described to you is actually the outward raiment, the outward revelation, the appearance of beings who hold sway in the cosmos. These beings reveal themselves as those whom we know in anthroposophic literature as the Exusiai. I have therefore often spoken of these Exusiai as revelations or manifestations, since by their inner nature they live in what streams in our sense organs towards our interior during sleep. The life and activity of these beings of the higher hierarchies whom we call the Exusiai is revealed in this streaming flow.

Now with the same means by which we can observe these manifestations of the etheric substance of the human senses stirring into such living activity particularly during sleep, we can perceive also how this inward streaming and shining continues further inwards. In our waking life we may see some shining object far off, and we can turn our gaze towards it to discover where it lies within our eye's field of vision. In the same way, we can look inwards, instead of outwards, and trace the etheric flow streaming from our senses, flowing and shining from them; and doing so, it will not be long before we encounter something else. The gentle phosphorescence that emanates from the eyes, the musical resonance that emanates locally from the ears, the streaming currents of warmth that pass inwards from the whole surface of the skin, all this very quickly passes over into an organically enclosed etheric system. Observing a waking person we can see the activity of his etheric body, and his whole physical body too, though involved now in a somewhat different activity than I described for the state of sleep. When he is awake we see this etheric activity expanding a little beyond the confines of the person's physical body. Now, though, in sleep, we see what streams, shines and surges inwards from his senses: a kind of inward-extending, bowl-like replica of the human being.[28]

In life after death, the musical-astral aspect of our life on earth seeks its connection with the corresponding regions of devachan.

And the astral body lives here in the tone world already, forming it in melody and harmony which we do not find in the external physical world because what we experience after death is already present in our astral body. As you know, this astral body that we bear within us lives with us only for a while after death, and then we divest ourselves of it too. Nevertheless this astral body bears an intrinsically musical element in itself. But it does so in a way governed by its experiences of the living element of air here between birth and death. We need the air if we wish to have a medium for our musical experience.

Arriving at the stage after death when we divest ourselves of the astral body, we also divest ourselves of everything that reminds us of musical experience here in earthly life. Yet at this cosmic moment the musical element transforms into the music of the spheres. We become independent of the musical element we experience through the air, and are raised instead into the music of the spheres. What we experience here as music through the medium of air becomes the music of the spheres in a higher region. Its reflection enters the element of air, grows denser, becomes what we impress into our astral body, what we elaborate and, as long as we still have our astral body, what we continue to experience. After death we divest ourselves of the astral body. And then—please forgive the banal expression—our musical nature swoops up into the music of the spheres. And so we have in music and poetry a prefiguring of our world after death, our existence there.[29]

3. THE ART OF MUSIC—'MUSICA INSTRUMENTALIS'

Rudolf Steiner's comments on the art of music are largely suggestions and stimulus for directions in which composers might move in future. In one of his first lectures on music (3 December 1906) he asks where the artistically formed tone originates and what it relates to in the world. His answer to this question opens up a great panorama that encompasses the human being and his diverse bodies or aspects, as well as the 'Spirit Land' of devachan.

For those who have reflected on this subject, music, the element of music, has always occupied a somewhat mysterious place amongst the arts. On the one hand it is the most easily comprehensible to our life of soul, our human sensibility; but on the other, its effect and the way it works is hard to fathom. If we compare music with the other arts we have to say that the latter can all look outwards to a model. When a sculptor wishes to create the figure of Zeus or Apollo, he bases this idealized image on the actual human world around him. The same is true of painting. Today in painting there is even a movement to reproduce reality exactly as it is perceived. Poetry likewise seeks to reflect reality. But if you try to apply this theory to music it will scarcely lead anywhere. And so we have to ask where the artistically formed tone originates and what it relates to in the world.

[...]

When a musician composes he cannot imitate. He must draw forth from his soul the themes of his musical creativity. We can discover where he draws these from if we point to the worlds that our senses do not perceive. Here we must imitate, really, the way higher worlds are constituted. Human beings are capable of accessing higher capacities that otherwise slumber within the soul. Just as someone born blind may gain vision through an operation, so the human being's inner organs can be opened to enable him to perceive higher worlds.

When we develop capacities that otherwise slumber within us, and begin to develop the soul through meditation, concentration and so on, we gradually raise ourselves to a higher condition. The first thing we experience is that our dream-life begins to change in a particular way. If we can shut out all our memories of the external sense world and other experiences, yet retain our inner content of soul, our dream world begins to acquire great regularity. Then, when we wake up it is as if we were rising out of a surging cosmic ocean. We know that we have experienced something new, as if emerging from an ocean of light and colour we have never known in the physical world. Our dream experiences acquire increasing clarity. We can recall things and beings in this world of light and colour that differ from other objects in that we can pass through them, that they offer us no resistance. We learn to know a sum of beings and entities whose element, whose bodies, are colours. These beings reveal and embody themselves in colour. Gradually the human being extends his awareness over this world and on awakening remembers that he lived and acted within it. The next step is that he takes this world with him into waking life. Then we gradually learn to see what we call the human astral body. We experience a world that is far more real than the ordinary physical world. The physical world is a kind of condensation, crystallized out of the astral world. In this way a person develops two levels of consciousness: that of daily waking life and dream consciousness.

A person attains a still higher stage when he becomes able to entirely transform the state of complete unconsciousness into one that is conscious. The adept or esoteric pupil learns to acquire continuity of consciousness for parts of the night—the periods without dream that are usually entirely unconscious. He learns to become conscious in a world of which he otherwise knows nothing. This new world is not one of light and colour but first announces itself as a world of tone. In this state of consciousness he acquires the capacity to hear spiritually, to hear combinations and multiplicities of tone that are inaudible to the physical ear. This is the world called devachan.

Now it should not be thought, when he first begins to hear the spiritually sounding world, that he no longer retains the world of light and colour. The tone world is also pervaded by light and colour, though these belong to the astral world. But the most intrinsic element of the world of devachan is the surging ocean of tones. From this realm of the continuity of consciousness, again a person can bring back the element of sonority and thereby also hear tones in the physical world. Everything in the physical world is founded upon a tone. Every face embodies certain tones of devachan. All objects are ultimately and intrinsically rooted in a spiritual tone; and in his deepest being each person is a spiritual tone too. This is why Paracelsus said that the kingdoms of nature are the letters and the human being is the word formed from them. Whenever we fall asleep, become unconscious, our astral body emerges from the physical body. Then, although unconscious, we live in the world of spirit, and the spiritual tones resonate in our soul.

Every morning we awaken again from the world of the music of the spheres, re-entering the physical world from a realm of harmonies. Given that the human soul has an existence in devachan between two physical embodiments, we can say that during the night the soul also lives and revels in a flowing sea of tone as the element from which its fabric is in fact woven, which is its true home.

The composer transforms into physical tone the rhythm, harmonies and melodies that impress themselves into his astral body during the night. Unconsciously the musician draws on the world of spirit as his exemplar and realizes this in the physical tones he composes. This is the mysterious connection between music here in the physical realm and our hearkening to spiritual music during the night.

When a light shines on someone, a shadow is cast: this is not the person himself. Thus the music created in the physical realm is the shadow, the real shadow or reflection of a much higher music of devachan. The archetype, the 'original' of the music is in devachan, while physical music is only a reflection of this spiritual reality.

Having established this, now let us try to understand how music affects us. The basis for esoteric investigation here is the knowledge that we can see the human being in terms of physical body, etheric body, astral body and I. The etheric body is an etheric archetype of the physical body. A still finer body, related to the etheric body and tending towards the astral body, is the sentient body. Within these three levels or aspects we see the soul, which is initially connected with the sentient body. Now the sentient body is as it were integrated with the sentient soul, the latter embedded in it. Like a sword in its sheath, the sentient body and sentient soul form a single whole. We also have our rational or mind soul, our 'sensibility soul', and, as a still higher aspect, the consciousness soul. This latter is associated with the Spirit Self or manas. When we are asleep, the sentient body lies in the bed with the physical and etheric body, while our higher aspects, thus also the sentient soul, are in the world of devachan. In physical space we feel all other beings to be outside us whereas in devachan we do not feel this separation; there they permeate us and we are in them. This is why all esoteric schools have spoken of the sphere of devachan, and the astral sphere too as the world of 'permeation'.

Alive in the world of surging tones, we ourselves are imbued with these tones. Returning from this world of devachan, our own consciousness soul, mind soul and sentient soul are infused with the resonances of devachan: we possess them within us. We bear them back with us as we penetrate the physical world again. Having absorbed these resonances, they can work back from the sentient soul upon the sentient body and the etheric body. Having brought them back with us from devachan, we can transfer these reverberations to our own etheric body. The nature of the etheric and sentient body is constituted largely of the same elements, spiritual tone and spiritual resonances. The etheric body is lower in nature than the astral body, but the *activity* arising in the etheric body is of a higher kind than that of the astral body. Human development involves our I transforming what we already possess, first the astral body into manas, then the etheric body into buddhi, and then the physical body into atma. Since the astral body is the finest in nature, we need the least energy or effort to work upon it transformatively. The strength we need to transform the etheric body has to be drawn from the world of devachan, and that required to transform the physical body must come from the higher world of devachan. We can work upon the astral body, however, with the powers of the astral world itself, while only the powers of the world of devachan can transform the etheric body and those of the higher world of devachan the physical body.

During the night we draw from the world of streaming tones the strength to pass them to our sentient body and etheric body. Our ability to be musically creative, and listen to music, is due to the fact that we already possess these sonorities in the sentient body. When we wake up in the morning we are not aware that we have absorbed tones during the night, but when we listen to music we sense that we bear these impressions of the world of spirit within us. When a clairvoyant listens to music, he can see how the tones stream and flow, how they engage with the more solid substance of the etheric body and make it resonate. This gives us a sense of well-being, due to the sense of vanquishing the etheric body through our astral body. This experience becomes strongest when we succeed in overcoming the etheric body's intrinsic nature. The etheric body is always resonating up into the astral body, but when we listen to music this first impresses itself on the astral body which consciously imparts them to the etheric body and overcomes the tones that are already present there. This gives rise to the sense of well-being when we listen to music as well as when we compose it. In certain musical sonorities something is passed from the astral body to the etheric body, which thus receives and acquires new tones. A kind of conflict arises between the sentient body and the etheric body. If these tones are strong enough to overcome the etheric body's own tones, we get cheerful music in the major key. Music in the major key characterizes music where the sentient body overcomes the etheric body, whereas music in the minor key shows the etheric body to be victorious over the sentient body. The etheric body resists the resonances of the sentient body.

When we live in a musical element, we dwell in a reflection of our spiritual home. In the shadow of the spirit the soul finds its highest elation, its most intimate connection with the primordially human element. And this is why music can affect the plainest souls. The most ordinary person can feel in music the echo of what they experienced in devachan: they feel themselves at home. And on each such occasion they sense that they originate in a different world.

It was this intuitive insight that made Schopenhauer accord music a central position amongst the arts. He said that in music we perceive the beating heart of the will.

In music we feel the echoes of what lives and weaves in the inmost nature of things, and is so deeply related to us. Since feelings are the soul's inmost element, and bear an affinity with the world of spirit, and because tone is the element in which the soul intrinsically moves, it lives there in a world where the corporeal mediators of feeling are no longer present, but where the feelings still live. The archetype of music is in the spiritual realm, whereas the archetypes of the other arts lie in the physical world itself. When we listen to music we feel well-being because these tones we hear correspond and accord with what we have experienced in the world of our spiritual home.[30]

When we consider how the composer is connected with his unconscious experiences in devachan, we can ask about the significance of musical composition, both now and in future, for a composer who has embarked on the path of schooling. The com-

poser's spirit and soul experiences as he pursues this path of schooling can come to expression in a music of the future.

Artistic creativity is an ever-developing need; and if we seek the spiritual foundation for the furtherance of such artistic efforts we must look for them in the account of initiation processes as described in *Occult Science* following descriptions of the Saturn, Sun, Moon and Earth stages of evolution, as well as the briefer outline given there of further evolutionary stages of Jupiter, Venus and Vulcan. These initiation processes are initially ones that occur unseen within us, but as we meet them today in their infancy we can regard them as the beginning of important transformations of human life on earth in future. After all, if we consider human life on earth with somewhat deeper feelings, we can easily get a sense that this life of ours, in so far as we are conscious of it, makes us seem like an orphan in the cosmos, an abandoned orphan, or perhaps a lost wanderer in the cosmos.

In the daily awareness of our waking life we do not know, after all, how what arose through Saturn, Sun and Moon existence came about; we do not know what lives in us, nor what will become of us in the future states of Jupiter, Venus and Vulcan existence. Without understanding our origins and our future, we wander by the side of an earthly abyss. Sometimes we may feel safe and secure in our human consciousness, and also secure in our future, but with our earthly apprehension neither past nor future can be measured in objective terms. But when we learn the guidelines embodied in the laws of initiation, we can inwardly apprehend something that leads and guides us in a surer direction. In ancient times such initiation was seen as a certain inheritance from the gods, a naturally endowed atavistic clairvoyance which, however, as we live on into the future, will increasingly encompass us and must shape our inner life of soul anew.

Certainly, this path of initiation has two aspects. One is that we acquaint ourselves through initiation with the riddles of life, entering into a spiritual apprehension and experience of existence. The other, however, is what we can call the more subjective aspect, which unfolds more inwardly as we pursue this path. This is at the same time what most alarms people since it does in fact represent an uncomfortable part of inner experience, from which we may shy away. Someone who seeks to gradually enter into initiation will find that it involves a spectrum of inner experience that is vast and detailed. On the path of initiation a continual fluctuation occurs as we pass through all manner of diverse experiences of self-conquering, release, hindrance and deliverance. We have to pass through everything that can make our own soul seem suddenly foreign to us, as if it had suddenly plunged into an abyss where it must feel eternally lost and can never rediscover what it once acquired at a former period of life. Something like an infinite dismay and grief for the loss of an existence that previously seemed secure can overwhelm us—as if our soul is on the verge of fracturing and fragmenting, dissolving into infinite diversity, vanishing into all the beings and entities of which the cosmos is composed. Then again comes a sense of having to wander through the beings of the universe, first becoming related to one then departing from it and finding affinity with the next—as I described in my book *The Threshold of the Spiritual World.* There I wrote of experiences that are always connected with painful self-privations, painful loneliness. And when the soul experiences the most radical transformation of all, it must decide to embrace what can be expressed as loss of the self for a while, as repulsing ourselves yet retaining a sense of trust that, in losing ourselves, in pushing away from ourselves beings who reside in the breadths of the divine hierarchies, we will nevertheless be preserved and at last rediscover ourselves. This is to pass through multiple births and deaths as we undergo the inner experiences that lead us to initiation.

Ultimately this involves a terrifying journey through all the powers necessary in the non-earthly cosmos but not part of ordinary life on earth. When Lucifer and Ahriman introduce these powers wrongfully into earthly life, they become the forces of evil, along with everything that they embody as tumultuous, destructive, engulfing powers throughout the cosmos. In passing through this stage we feel ourselves to be nothing but an instrument through which spiritual beings speak, where symbolically we become in our entirety what our larynx, as one part of us, brings to expression, become as it were the larynx of divine, spiritual beings, feel ourselves resting in the all-pervading divine Word. And then comes the condition when, in future, this sense will culminate in a universal experience of the divine will and activity at work in the cosmos.

But I am describing only certain states amongst an infinite range of what the soul undergoes. In *Knowledge of Higher Worlds* or more descriptively in *The Threshold of the Spiritual World*, you can find accounts of how the soul can find its way into all these conditions and, with each one, climb a little higher upon the path of initiation, come one step further into the world of spirit. Yes, everything through which the soul passes as it approaches initiation is consciously undergone and experienced, and this is why this path of knowledge is both so painful and so redemptive. But long, long before a person can consciously find his way into the stages of the initiation path as I describe them he can give pictorial expression to them to some degree—and this occurs through music. Ultimately true music is existence that unfolds in sonorities, an unfolding process of life in tones as an outward picture or representation of what the soul consciously undergoes through initiation.

If we stay within the confines of our ordinary, daily life we will not easily be able to accomplish what can be called an immersion of the I in the astral body, as we described this yesterday. Doing this in the right way, plunging down into the astral world with the I so that this submersion is at the same time an immersion in the divine world, is precisely what initiation involves. But we have an image of this in what happens when works of music approach us, either as composers ourselves or as listeners. When we give ourselves up to music either creatively or as an audience, we divest ourselves of the I. We suppress the I, but at the same time we offer it up to all the divine, spiritual beings who will work upon our astral body when we rise to Jupiter existence.

And so, you see, we are now entering into a reflection on the art of music that connects us at the same time with our human future. It seems almost immodest to say that a creative musician is actually called upon to perfect himself increasingly, to enter ever deeper into the world; and that the musical compositions so far created and present in the world remain attempts, more or less, however great and magnificent they are, however brilliant. They are attempts in a sense, efforts to approach something infinitely more significant in the musical compositions of the future. In future, musical creativity, the composing of musical works, will be able to receive the most important stimulus as people allow themselves increasingly to engage with the inner character of the path of initiation and become more deeply acquainted with it.

A time will come when people no longer experience as they do today accounts that can be given of the path of initiation, but when instead descriptions of the soul's experiences and travails, its bliss and deep disappointments, become fully vivid in their experience rather than intellectual apprehension. Then the human soul will be sensitive to such a degree that it will first be shaken to its very depths by sympathy with the destinies of all the non-human beings that participate in the events unfolding in the cosmos, will vividly experience inner turmoil, privations and deliverances that will drive it to express in sonorities what can be experienced in such accounts and descriptions of the path of initiation. In future times there will be human beings who feel descriptions of the path of initiation as intense experiences of what today seems so abstract; they will experience these things far more intensely than is the case for us today in our outward, physical modes of perception. For those who can feel the truth of things described in relation to the path of initiation, a moment will arrive when they say, 'Now I feel that what I experience in this way no longer connects me with the surrounding natural world in which I live on the earth but instead with what pulses and lives in the cosmos. Oh, I cannot merely feel and experience this but I can and must sing it, compose it in music!'

In an account such as this we have a pointer to what spiritual science should become for humankind. It should kindle the life of the human soul rather than remaining theoretical. It should not be knowledge merely. The science of the spirit should live in the soul, engaging all the soul's powers and making us different human beings. Or rather we should make *ourselves* into different human beings by dedicating ourselves to spiritual science.[31]

Both in 1915,[32] and between 1920 and 1924, Rudolf Steiner spoke on many occasions of the future development of music, seeing this as connected with a deepened experience of the single tone arising through spiritual-scientific schooling. He made extensive remarks on this while answering questions on 29 and 30 September 1920. This was in relation to three lectures given by Paul Baumann on 'Music and Eurythmy in Education' on 27, 28 and 29 September during the first course of the School of Spiritual Science (GA 322) that was held at the opening of the Goetheanum.[33] After the lecture by Paul Baumann on 29 September 1920, Steiner was asked about an expansion of the classical tone system. He did not wish to answer this in isolation, however, but placed it in the context of a deepened experience of the single tone.

We have heard about an expansion of the tone system, and various speakers here, I believe, are interested in this, including musicians and composers.

Now, the whole question in my view is connected with another, which is perhaps less easy to grasp than is usually thought. What I would first like to do is address a question of my own to those who have participated in this discussion about expanding the tone system.[34]

The following comments by Steiner reveal that his listeners could not immediately relate to the question of a deepened experience of the single tone as he describes it.

I believe that there is a clearly discernible tendency today, particularly amongst people with a strong musical sensibility, to enter more deeply into the tone itself. One can either stay closer to the surface of a tone, or penetrate more deeply into it.

And so now I would like to ask those who were part of our earlier discussions to tell me whether it makes any sense to them if I say that modern musical experience is increasingly tending towards a view that splits the tone, so that in a sense we question the single tone about the degree to which it already is, or is not, melody. Can you relate to this idea at all? You see, we cannot really speak of an expansion of the tonal system at all unless we have a proper foundation for discussing it.

Earlier, remarks were made about noise. The whole discussion about noise can probably only be resolved if we first set out the foundations as I suggested. For example—and I am not sure if these things are already a common subjective experience or not—I assume that the gentleman who spoke here for a long time, and dwelt on the subject of noises, inclines to the view that a melody can be perceived within the tone. If so, I understand him; I fully understand how he enters into an individual tone or into separate sounds that another hears only as noise. By listening to the depths of the tone, however, he will find something there that then gives rise to noise but, seeking this out, can allow something musical to arise from it. Someone else who does not plunge down into these depths of the tone will fail to understand or relate to this.

This morning, Dr Husemann pointed out that in another respect, too, modern humanity faces a situation where the persona is gradually splitting apart. And so it also seems that there are already a fair number of people today who simply have a different experience of the single tone than very highly trained musicians of whatever school. This is connected with the other question that was asked, about how spiritual science relates to all of this.

Now I'd like to ask this specific question. Does it make any sense to say that in some circumstances the single tone can already be experienced as a melody if one plumbs its depths? If one distinguishes parts of it, partial tones, whose relationship, whose harmony can in turn become a kind of melody?

Paul Baumann: It was also clear from my lecture that I relate noise to harmonics, and thus to compressed or consolidated melody. Can we regard a ringing noise as a condensed melody, perhaps harmony, but one which we experience musically? In reality every noise is doubtless musical but we do not need to see it as artistic. We can't distinguish this but can feel very clearly in musical tones that there is an aspect here of something especially musical, something of the mobility of things; that we can clearly distinguish the merely musical tone, which as such is not heard, from the element within which it very clearly resonates.

No, I didn't mean that. I was speaking specifically now of an expansion of our capacity to experience tone itself; in other words, when experiencing a tone, to enter into its depths or, if you like, to draw these forth from the tone so that one really experiences something already in the tone itself.

Paul Baumann: And I meant distinguishing what one needs in the art of music, what is harmonious, which one likewise employs to feel something musically active in things.

No, that is not what I was saying; I was referring rather to what one experiences in a *single* tone, without any objective correlative. One splits the tone itself and recreates it again as a synthesis. I'm speaking of this as direct experience. In olden times people assigned the tone to the tone spirit. In popular terms: in the Passau mystery play of 1250 the devil appears at the very outset before the play itself begins. He is introduced as the Tempter, and to create the right mood for this the devil has to blow into a fire alarm horn. This is so shrill and piercing that all take fright. That is the epitome of this tone spirit I am talking of.

A few more opinions are voiced.

None of these things are what I meant—experiencing in a *single* tone something that appears as melody. When a tone is struck or sounded, a melody actually reverberates from it.

Dr Stein: It seems to me we need to distinguish between hearing a tone and our sense of tone. In hearing a tone I feel something particularly deep, and, when I feel a pain or get a fright, this feeling element passes . . .

It is not my aim now to define things that simply exist but to discern whether we live in a time of transition in relation to people's experience of tone, so that it actually becomes something else. Today it seems to me that tone is still regarded as an entity connected with others, existing in a melody and so on; but it is also possible to enter the depths of a tone, perhaps even to search for something that underlies it. We can't really have a fruitful discussion before this aspect is considered.

Further opinions are voiced.

If you hear a tone being held for a long time, for instance at the beginning of the *Freischütz* overture, you can have a sense that I may be able to convey pictorially. The tone can be seen as half an arc—I mean this as an image; and then I would need to draw something like thin nerves attached to it, emerging from it. This arc or curve would give one a sense of the tone entering here then coming out again the other side, emerging again as nerves and veins, so that we have a kind of inner movement that is at one moment on one side of this half arc and at another on the other side. Perhaps one could express this dynamically too by saying that one puts in a greater intensity and then withdraws it again.

Further comments.

I have spoken of holding a note a long time only so that we can better observe this. To hold a long note might sometimes also make it possible for us to observe changes in the tone. I am not speaking now of some kind of graph that can be drawn in this way, but a curve or arc that can be drawn horizontally thus.

Further comments: . . . Is this to do with the intensity?

That is why I said: enter more deeply into the tone!

Longer comments by a participant.
Herr van Pals describes his experiences with a single tone; prelude to the poems of Jacobowski. A tone, drawn from the poem itself, its content; there was no wish whatever to depart again from this tone; it was there and could equally well have remained there, was a melody in itself—I only departed from it because you couldn't have played that one note for half an hour.

Now we have discussed this matter for a while, I would just like to say that sometimes new developments emerge in very imperfect ways in the early stages. For instance, Expressionism has appeared in some pretty dubious forms at present, yet this should not lead people to be critical of all Expressionist art but only of its inadequacies in some respects. There is certainly more to it than as yet meets the eye, and this will emerge and become very significant. In respect of the further development of music, too—in a way that closely resembles our efforts in painting to feel our way into the colours and to paint out of colour—this living into the tone signifies the very beginning of further developments. I quite understand that its early manifestations may not be looked on favourably. That doesn't matter. But I would like to know how we can understand composers such as Debussy if we do not regard them as—however vague—forerunners of something of this kind that lies in the future. If we can acknowledge this, we can discover that it opens up a certain possibility for us to compose in a different way; and this will mean that the relationship between composer and orchestral player becomes much freer; that the player who reproduces the composition is far less constrained and can himself become far more creative, having much more scope to be so. But this only becomes possible in music if the tone system is expanded so that one can really have the variations that are necessary for this, the possibility for very marked variations. I could imagine for example that what a composer offers in future might be far more open, in the form of suggestions and possibilities; and because of this the player would need far more variants, far more tones to express what is needed. If one finds one's way into the depths of the tone, one can distribute or assign it in the most varied ways, extrapolating it in turn into neighbouring tones. In this way a fluid, versatile musical life would arise. I can only give brief outlines. We could go on talking all night, but we had better not since we're meeting again tomorrow. But this will give rise to a much more versatile musical life. And we can say that it really is possible already to have an inkling of this more versatile musical experience.[35]

The discussion continues the next day.

Now I have just become aware of a difference of opinion in relation to what I meant yesterday by entering more deeply into the tone.

I did not mean a sequence of tones that remain present and create chords together, which are then seen as one tone. I did not mean this, but rather that today, in a way simply inherent in humanity's evolution, what a great many people have hitherto experienced as a single tone up to our own times they will now begin to experience as inwardly differentiated and split. In a sense therefore people will enter more deeply into the tone or below it, passing through it and beyond it to a different tone. The original tone, with two neighbouring tones derived from its alteration will give us three tones as a modified main tone. It is then a somewhat different tone. And the new tones thus created, which in a sense produce a small melody, will be such that we see that one of them must be pushed away upwards and the other downwards. But by doing so we find that we arrive at microtones that we are not used to in our conventional keys, tones they simply do not possess. And in this way, I believe, an expansion of our tonal system will be inevitable.

And it is also true to say, in a certain sense, that the opposite process to this is what gave rise to our modern tone system. Modern tonality only arose through overlaying of all kinds of tonal awareness. These keys of ours would not be immediately comprehended in certain former eras.

And so I believe that something is changing in our whole tonal awareness today, and also that the sometimes very grotesque, experimental forms of music now appearing are prefiguring the emergence of something new. You see, I have to say that either I completely fail to understand Debussy or I understand him, rather, as prefiguring something of this deeper immersion in the tone, a premonition of this. The musical sensibility apparent in Debussy is after all of a quite different kind even than, for instance, in Wagner.[36]

Below Steiner makes some aphoristic comments on the art of singing (1916) and the question of musical instruments (1923).

Ahriman has compressed or condensed speech and song from the entirety of human nature. When this comes to be rightly understood, something of enormous importance will arise from it for the way we actually live. Firstly, in relation to vocal training, the principle will emerge that the student must become aware of the part which the etheric body plays in singing: in a sense how tones are continually guided into the etheric body. Only when account is really taken of this involvement of the etheric body in singing will the transformative impulse arise in its teaching that must necessarily follow from our principles. In practical terms this will become apparent in the fact that teachers of singing will increasingly call upon the student to focus less intently on the physical organs of the voice and instead develop more awareness within what, if you like, adjoins these physical organs. When singing, we must have a sense not so much of the movement of the vocal organs but of how the air is moving within and around them. Proper insight into the spiritual-scientific principles of singing training will help us to emancipate a conscious experience of the tone in the air from an experience of the tone in the vocal organ.[37]

But now let us ask about the general musical evolution of the human being. This originates in an experience of the spirit, in making the spiritual present in the tone, in the musical configuration of tone. The spiritual is gradually lost, leaving tone configurations behind. Later the human being connects these with the word as a residue of spirit; and what he formerly possessed as imaginations, the instruments, he then develops physically, making these instruments from physical materials. Musical instruments have all been drawn from the world of spirit in so far as they actually invoke a musical mood. By making musical instruments, the human being filled the places left empty by his inability to see the spirit any longer. He placed his physical musical instruments into these spaces.

So you can see that in the field of music we can be more aware than elsewhere of the transition into the materialistic age. Where musical instruments now resound, spiritual entities once stood. They are gone, have vanished from perception that is no longer clairvoyant as it was in ancient times. If we wish to possess the objective reality of music, however, we need something that is not present in external nature. Since the natural world around us does not offer a correlate for musical experience, we need our musical instruments.

The musical instruments are basically a clear reflection of the fact that we experience music with and in our whole being. That we experience music through the head is shown in the wind instruments. The string instruments are a living testimony to the fact that what we experience in our breast comes to expression especially in our arms. And all percussion instruments, or the transition from string to percussion instruments, reveal musical experience in our limb system. Now whereas blowing has a much more intimate relationship to melody, string instruments embody a relationship with harmony. And percussion, everything connected with a more interior rhythm, is related to the rhythmic element which pervades the whole of us. An orchestra is actually a single human being, as long as it has no piano.

Why so? Well, the musical instruments have been drawn down as it were from the world of spirit. But the piano has been conceived and created only in the physical world, and its tones are set alongside each other in a purely abstract way. Any flute or fiddle has descended from a higher world, but a piano is like a philistine and no longer contains a higher being. The piano is a philistine instrument. It is fortunate that it exists, though, for otherwise a philistine would be deprived of music. The piano has arisen from a materialistic experience of music, and therefore one can most easily use it to awaken music within matter. Matter itself alone has been employed so that the piano could become an expression of music. But one has to acknowledge that the piano is a very benevolent instrument. Without it, you see, we would have had to draw on the help of spirit in music education from the very outset in our materialistic age. But it is the instrument that will need to be overcome in music, really. We will have to free ourselves from our awe of the piano if we wish to have truly musical experience.

And it has to be said that it is a grandiose experience when a musician who lives in music through and through, someone like Bruckner, plays on the piano. When Bruckner plays, the piano vanishes from the room! It seems one hears other instruments, and the piano itself is forgotten. Bruckner achieves this. This can show that something truly spiritual was living in him, albeit in a very instinctive way: a spiritual element that underlies all music.[38]

In a key lecture on music, 'Human Expression in Tone and Word' (2 December 1922), Steiner elaborates the spiritual, soul and physical aspect of music as illustrated by song. This lecture deals specifically with the phenomenon of music, also in the realm after death. His thought pictures here can be seen as meditative content for deepening musical creativity and composition.

As we know, the physical form of the human being is the outcome of magnificent spiritual activity which we accomplish together with the beings of higher worlds between death and rebirth. But what we shape and configure during that time, the spiritual germ in a sense of our future physical organization on earth, does not in itself contain the capacity to stand upright. This capacity is one that informs us only after we are born, when we integrate ourselves into the reciprocal forces of earthly existence. In pre-birth existence, orientation does not signify what it later comes to mean on earth when we walk or stand. There, rather, it signifies the relationship we have with the beings of the Angeloi and Archangeloi, and thus with the beings of the higher hierarchies—with the one more than the other depending on which being one feels more drawn towards. That is the state of balance in worlds of spirit, and is something we lose in a sense when we descend to earth. In our mother's womb we are really neither in the states of equilibrium of our spiritual life nor yet in those of our earthly life. We have departed from the former without yet entering into the latter.

It is similar with language. The speech we have here on earth is fully adapted to earthly conditions, for it is an expression of our earthly thoughts. These earthly thoughts contain earthly knowledge, earthly wisdom to which language adapts during our life on earth. In pre-earthly existence we have a language too, though one that does not emerge from within, primarily conducted on the breath, but which instead follows the spiritual inbreath, Inspiration. In pre-earthly life it corresponds to what the inbreath is for us here. This is a life in communion with the universal Logos, a life in the cosmic Word, the cosmic language that gives rise to all things.

We depart from this life in the cosmic language when we descend again to earth, uniting ourselves here with what initially serves to express our thoughts, earthly thoughts, human reason, human communication between all who live on earth. The same is true of the thoughts we have here, our thinking. Thinking is adapted to earthly conditions. In pre-earthly life we live in the activity of weaving cosmic thoughts.

If we first consider our middle system, our human speech, we can say that it encompasses something key to earthly culture, earthly civilization. Speech brings people together here on earth, forms the bridge through which one person finds their way to another. This is how souls connect with each other. In speech we feel that we have something of core importance here on earth, as the earthly reflection of life in the Logos, the cosmic Word. This is why it is very interesting indeed to consider the connection between what we wrestle to express in speech here on earth with the metamorphosis this speech undergoes in the other, pre-earthly realm. If we consider this relationship, we are led from speech sound and musical tone to our inner organization.

And at this moment it is rather fitting that I can include comments on human expression in tone and word in the cosmological observations we have been engaged in for several weeks now. During this time we have had the great pleasure of hearing such fine, outstanding singing here at our Goetheanum. And today therefore, in a sense as expression of my inner satisfaction at this beautiful artistic event, I wish to say a few words specifically about the connection between the speech and musical utterances of earthly human beings and the correspondence of this with our life in the world of spirit.

If we consider the human organization as it appears to us here on earth, it is entirely a reflection of the spirit. Everything here, not just our human characteristics but all that surrounds us in the world of nature, is a reflection of the spirit. When we speak or sing, this is an outward expression of our whole organism, our body, soul and spirit, and an expression inwards too, towards our own self. We are in a sense entirely contained in the sounds and tones we express. The degree to which this is so only becomes apparent if we grasp in greater detail what we are when we speak or sing.

Let us start with speech. As the human being evolved, speech really emerged from what was originally song. The further back we go into prehistory, the closer speech comes to resemble recitation or chant and, earliest of all, song. And in very ancient times of humanity's evolution on earth, human utterance in speech and song was not separate but one and the same thing. We can say that primordial human speech was primordial song. Now if we look at modern speech which has very much distanced itself from pure song and has assumed a strongly prosaic element, an intellectual element, we find two distinct aspects in language, consonants and vowels. Everything we utter in speech is composed of either consonants or vowels. The consonantal aspect is really entirely based on our finer bodily structures. If we say B or P or L or M, this is due to the fact that something in our body has a specific shape or form. It is not always the case that, in speaking of these forms, we must speak only of the vocal organs, which are only the culmination of related processes. When we produce a speech sound or a musical tone, our whole organism is involved in this; and what occurs in our organs of speech and singing is only the final culmination of what occurs in our whole organism. The form of our human organism could therefore be regarded like this: all the consonants in a language are always variations on twelve primal consonants. In Finnish, for example, these twelve primordial consonants are more or less preserved in their pure form: eleven are very marked and only the twelfth has become a little unclear; it is however still clearly apparent in . . . [gap in text]. These twelve primordial consonants, if we grasp them correctly—each can be represented by a different form—can actually be composed together into the whole sculptural shape of the human organism. This is not at all metaphorical but we can actually say that the twelve primordial consonants embody the sculptural form of the human organism.

What is the real nature of this human organism? From the perspective of music it is in fact a musical instrument. Yes, you can basically understand musical instruments by regarding them, their shapes, whether the violin or another instrument, as built of consonants, as consonantal in nature. If we speak of the consonantal element we always have a feeling that resembles musical instruments. And the entirety, the harmony of all consonants, is embodied in the shape and form of the human organism.

And the vowel element is the soul who plays upon this instrument. So if you trace the consonants and vowels in every speech utterance and song, you find the self-expression of human nature. The human soul plays as vowel quality upon the consonants of the human being's corporeal instrument.

If we reflect on the speech and language that belongs to modern civilization and culture, our soul with its vowel element very strongly employs the head, brain and nerve organism. In earlier evolutionary periods this was not so in the same degree. I would like to sketch on the board what occurs here, somewhat schematically, very schematically.

Let us assume that we have in this way built our head and nerve organism [red]. These red lines represent the forces that pass along the nerves of the head. This is only a very limited view of what happens. Into this activity elaborated by the nerves, another activity enters, and comes about because we breathe in air. This air which we breathe in—this is all

schematic—enters directly through the spinal column here [yellow], and the breathing impetus creates a harmonious accord with the movements passing along the nerves. In your head, therefore, the stream of breath pushing through the spinal column towards the head continually encounters the activity of the nerves. We do not have a separate nerve activity and a separate breathing activity, but rather a resonant interplay between them in our head. Prosaic as people have become today in ordinary life, they place more value on the red forces here [see drawing]; they make greater use of their nervous system when they speak. One could say that they 'innervate' the instrument that shapes the vowel streams. This was not so in earlier times when people lived less in their nervous system but more in their respiration. This is why the primordial language was more songlike.

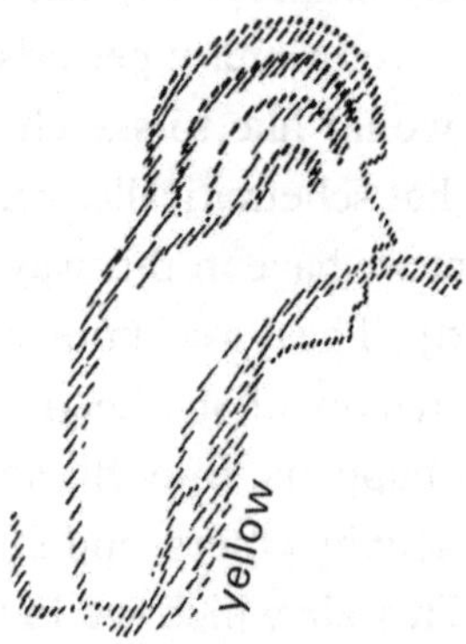

When people sing today they bring back to the stream of breath what in speech they otherwise accomplish through innervation by the nervous system; they consciously bring the second stream, that of the breath, into activity. This is the continuation of breathing into the head, directly activated when a tone is sung by infusing it with the vowel element. But when we sing we do not depart from the breath. Thus we bring a speech that has grown prosaic back into the poetic element, into the artistic element of rhythmic breathing.

Poets still try to have the rhythm of breathing in the way in which they shape the language of their poems. A composer of songs brings everything back into the breath, also into head breathing. In other words, what we have to undergo here on earth by adapting our speech to earthly conditions is in a sense reversed when we pass from speech to song. Song is in a sense a real memory, employing earthly means, of what we experienced in pre-birth existence. In our rhythmic system we are much closer to the world of spirit than in our thinking system. The thinking system of course influences our prosaic language.

When we utter vowels, we push towards the body something that really lives in the soul; the body offers its consonantal element as musical instrument. This can give you the sense that in every vowel there lives something that is inwardly alive, and that this is something one can intrinsically use, whereas the consonantal element continually yearns for vowel quality. The plastic corporeal instrument is really something dead if the vowel element, the soul, does not strike or stroke it. You can see this in small details. For instance, in certain central European dialects you have the word 'mir' in phrases such as 'es geht mir gut' [I am well]. When I was a small boy I could not understand that this word was written as it is. I always wrote it 'mia', since a yearning for the 'a' is implicit in the 'r'. When we understand the human organism as the harmony of the consonants we discover everywhere in it a yearning for vowel quality, or in other words for the soul. What is this due to?

This human organism as it has to establish its configuration here on earth must adapt to earthly conditions. It is configured in accordance with the dictates of earthly equilibrium, earthly forces, although it is originally shaped by the realm of spirit. What this means is something we can only recognize through spiritual-scientific research, and I will now try to clarify this schematically.

Let us assume that the soul's vowel expression [red] is expressed by meeting the resistance of consonantal quality [yellow], and that this consonantalism is shaped in accordance with earthly conditions.

If we now raise ourselves into the world of spirit as I described in my book *Knowledge of the Higher Worlds*, we first reach the realm of Imagination, imaginative perception. But here we have in the meantime lost the consonants, only retaining the vowels for now. In the realm of Imagination, after all, we have lost our physical body, we have lost the consonants. In the imaginative world we no longer have understanding of the consonants. To describe this condition adequately in words we have to say it consists entirely of vowels initially. So to begin with we lack the instrument, and we enter a world of tones that is still resonant with the most diverse nuances of vowels but in which the earth's consonants have been dissolved into vowels.

You will therefore find that in the words of languages that retained an affinity with primordial languages the things of the supersensible world are expressed in vowels. The word 'Yahveh' ('Yahweh') for instance did not have our 'y' and 'v' or 'w' but consisted only of vowels and was chanted or half-sung. Thus we find here a singing or chanting of vowels.

And if we pass from imaginative perception to Inspiration, where we directly receive the revelations of the spirit, then all consonants we have here on earth become something quite different. We lose the consonants. This is lost [with yellow covered over; see drawing below, lower yellow]; instead, in spiritual perception that can be acquired and investigated through Inspiration, something new starts to manifest—the spiritual counterparts of the consonants [see upper yellow].

But these spiritual counterparts to the consonants no longer live between the vowels but within them. Earthly language has consonants and vowels living alongside each other. As you rise into the world of spirit you lose the consonants and live in a singing world of vowels. But you yourself cease to sing: *it* sings. The world itself becomes cosmic song.

But this vowel expression is coloured soul-spiritually so that something lives in the vowels as the spiritual counterparts to the consonants. Here in earthly conditions you have the sound ah, and, say, a C sharp as tone in a particular octave. But as soon as we enter the world of spirit, instead of ah, or C sharp in a particular scale, we have countless tones that are inwardly diverse in quality—not just diverse octaves. You see it is something different if a being of the hierarchy of the Angeloi utters an ah or one from the hierarchy of Archangeloi, or a different being. Outwardly this is always the same but inwardly it is an ensouled expression. And so we can say that on earth we have our body [next drawing left, white], into which the vocalized tone resonates [red]. In the spiritual world, we have the vocalized tone [drawing right, red] and into this the soul [white] resonates and lives in it, so that the tone becomes the body of the soul.

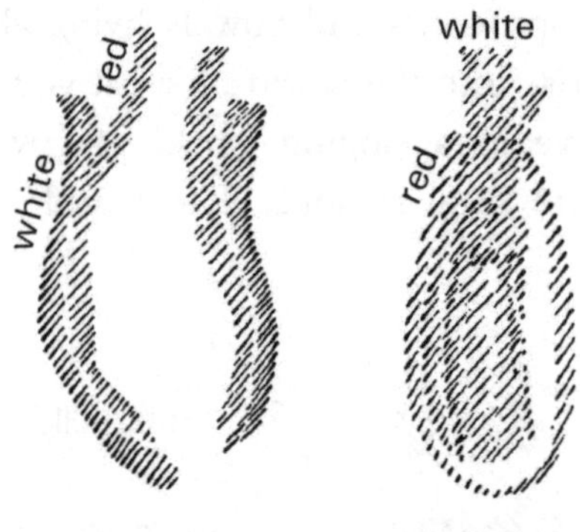

Now you are living in the cosmic music, in cosmic song; you are within the creative tone, the creative Word. If you picture the tone on earth, also the tone manifesting as speech sound, it lives in the air. But the physical idea that the shaping of air *is* the tone is really a naive one. Imagine you have a piece of ground here with a person standing on it. The ground is certainly not the person, but it has to be there so a person can stand on it. Otherwise the person couldn't be there. But this does not mean you will try to see the person as part of or in terms of the ground.

In the same way the air must be there so that the tone can gain a purchase. Just as a person stands on the ground, so the tone has its ground albeit in a somewhat more complicated way: it has its resistance in the air. Air has no more importance for tone than the ground does for the person standing on it. The tone seeks the air and the latter enables it to exist there. But the tone is something spiritual. Just as a person is something different from the ground, so the tone is different from the air upon which it stands. It stands too, though in a more complex, more manifold way.

Because we can only speak and sing on earth through the medium of air, the air shaped as tone is an earthly reflection of a soul-spiritual reality. The soul-spiritual nature of the tone really belongs to the supersensible world. And what lives here in the air is basically the body of the tone. It is scarcely surprising therefore that we rediscover tone in the world of spirit. Except that what originates in earthly conditions has been stripped away there: the earthly nature of consonants. The spiritual content of vowels, the intrinsic nature of tone, remains when we ascend into the world of spirit, but is then inwardly soul-permeated. Instead of being outwardly shaped by the consonantal realm, the tone is inwardly ensouled. And this goes hand-in-hand with the process of finding our way into the world of spirit altogether.

Now consider what happens when we pass through the gate of death. We soon leave the consonants behind us but instead experience the vowels more intensely, especially their intonations. But we no longer feel that singing comes from our larynx. Singing is all around us and we live in every tone. It is like this in the very first days after we have passed through the gate of death. We live really in the element of music, which is at the same time a speech element. In this musical element ever more of the world of spirit is revealed—an ensoulment.

As I said, this emergence into the world as we pass through the gate of death is at the same time a transition from the earthly world to the world of the stars.

In describing these things we seem to be speaking metaphorically but this pictorial element is completely real. Picture the earth to yourself, and the planets around it, firstly, then the fixed stars—which have rightly been called the 'zodiac' from time immemorial.

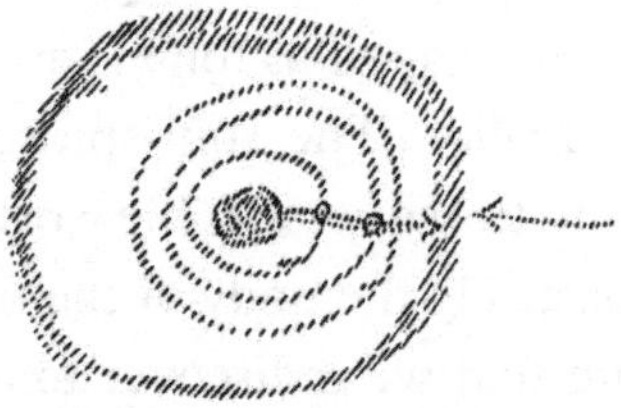

Standing on the earth we look up and see the planets and the fixed stars shining; we see their 'front' view, let us say, to pay due respect to our place on earth. Actually the Old Testament expresses this differently. Now as we distance ourselves from the earth after death, we gradually come to see both the planets and the fixed stars from behind. Instead of these points of light or planes of light that are seen from the earth, we see the corresponding spiritual presences. We find a whole world of spiritual beings. Looking back to Saturn, Sun, Moon or to Aries,

Taurus, and so on, from this other perspective we see spiritual entelechies.

In fact this vision is at the same time a hearing; just as one speaks of seeing the moon, Venus and so on from behind, or Aries, Taurus and so forth, so we can equally well speak of hearing the beings who have their dwelling in these cosmic bodies sound forth into cosmic breadths.

Now picture this whole configuration—certainly it does seem as if we are speaking metaphorically but this is not so, we are describing a reality. Picture the world of planets further away from you now, and nearer to you the zodiac with its constellations. All these cosmic bodies sing to you speakingly, speak singingly, and your perception is really a hearing of this speaking song, this singing speech.

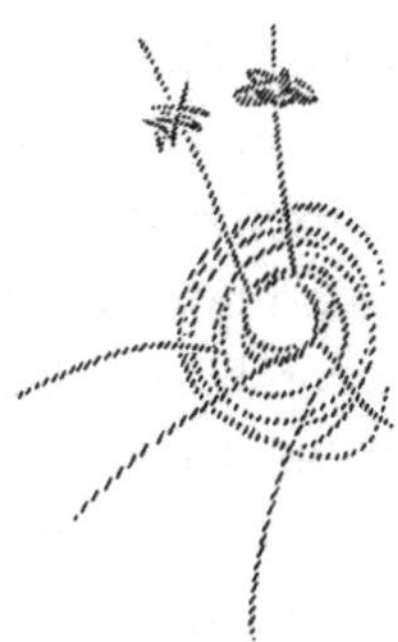

As you look towards Aries you have the impression of a soul consonant quality. Saturn may be behind Aries: a soul vowel quality. And in this soul vowel element that shines forth from Saturn into cosmic space lives the soul-spiritual consonant quality of Aries or Taurus. Here therefore you have the planetary sphere that sings forth its vowel quality to you into cosmic space, and you have the fixed stars which—

we can put it like this now—consonantally ensoul this song of the planetary sphere.

Picture this vividly: the fixed stars resting more, and behind them the wandering planets. As a wandering planet passes a fixed star configuration, not a tone but a whole world of tones resounds; and as it passes, say, from Aries to Taurus, a different tone world sounds forth.

And then a different tonality resounds as, let us say, Mars passes behind this star sign of Taurus.

You have in the heaven of fixed stars a wonderful cosmic instrument, behind which our planetary gods circulate as the players upon this instrument.

We can really say that speech, formed for earthly conditions—as walking develops in relation to earthly conditions from a cosmic, spiritual orientation—can be conveyed back into song, and that by doing so we incline again towards the pre-earthly existence out of which we were born. In fact we can say this of art in general, of our human artistic expression; we can say that it is human destiny. Rightly so, for as we enter earthly existence, find our way into earthly conditions, we must adapt to these conditions, but in art we take a step back, allowing the earthly to peter out around us and, through the backward step we take, approaching the realm of spirit and soul, the pre-earthly existence from which we emerged.

We fail to understand art if we do not find in it a yearning to experience the spirit, at least initially as revealed in beauty's appearance. Our imagination, which develops the realm of art, is really nothing other than a pre-earthly power of clairvoyance. As the tone lives on earth in the air, so what is really a spiritual reality in pre-earthly existence lives for the soul in an earthly reflection of spirit. When we speak we use our body to do so. The consonantal realm in us becomes the sculptural forms of our body. The soul uses the stream of breath, which does not merge with these solid forms, to play our corporeal instrument. But as earthly people who speak we can guide our nature towards the divine in one of two ways.

We can take the consonantal human organism and in a sense release it from its solid form, acquired through earthly forces of gravity or the chemical substances of nutrition; we can release the consonantal quality that pervades us! [. . .] If we dissect a human lung, we find chemical substances that can be chemically investigated. But these are not the lung. What is the lung? It is a consonant that has been spoken from the cosmos and has acquired form. We dissect a heart, and find it consists of cells whose chemical composition can be investigated. But they are not the heart, which is another consonant spoken from the cosmos. If we picture the twelve consonants spoken from the cosmos, we have, more or less, the human body before us.

In other words, if we have sufficient clairvoyant powers of vision to see the whole context of the consonants, we rediscover the full form of the human body. If we then withdraw the consonants from the human being again, we engage in the art of sculpture; and if on the other hand we withdraw from the human being the breath, which the soul uses to play upon this instrument in song, and whose nature is vowel, then we engage in music, singing.

By withdrawing the consonantal realm from the human being, form arises which you have to shape sculpturally. By withdrawing the vowel realm from the human being, song arises, the musical element, which must be sung. And so the human being as he stands before us is really the outcome of two cosmic arts: a sculpting cosmic art on the one hand, and a singing, musical cosmic art on the other. Two spiritual entelechies here merge their activity. One provides the instrument, the other plays upon it; one forms the instrument, the other plays it.

No wonder, then, that in ancient times, when people were still aware of these things, they invoked the greatest artist of all, Orpheus, who so powerfully commanded the realm of soul that he was able not only to employ the already formed human body as instrument but, through his tones, could also mould and shape unformed matter in forms that corresponded to the tones.

You will understand that to present such things one has to use words in a somewhat different way from how they are usually employed in our utilitarian times. Yet they are not meant merely symbolically or metaphorically. These are realities. These things are as I have described them, even if speech must sometimes be brought into greater flow to convey them than is usual or common today.[39]

In his last comments on music (in the lecture cycle Initiate Consciousness [True and False Paths in Spiritual Investigation] *in Torquay in August 1924), Steiner describes how one can approach an experience of the incarnation of the Christ being purely through shaping a certain sequence of intervals and their development in a rising major and descending minor mood.*

When a person attends feelingly—and he can—to research findings as I have indicated, so that the cosmic human being returns to us through insight into the organs, then the Christ can in a sense be understood in this return. When these results of esoteric research and perception, assimilated into initiate consciousness, arise in us as feeling, then in a sense the heavenly realm is revealed within the earthly through feeling within the consciousness I have described. And this occurs through art. In art a half-unconscious soul nature holds fast to what returns to human beings from the world of spirit on paths I characterized. This is why there have always been those predestined by their karma to hold the spirit fast in art in an earthly, material medium.

Our naturalistic art has departed from this. But every lofty height that art attains represents a spiritual element within the sensory world; or we could also say that it raises sensory reality into the sphere of the spirit. People value Raphael the painter so highly because he was able, to a degree unmatched by any other artist, to embody in sensory form something that raises itself to the spirit.

In human evolution in general there was a stream dedicated primarily to the visual arts. Today we must find new life again in the realm of the fine arts. But the immediate, elemental impulse for them belonged to past times. For a long time now, for centuries, the other impulse has been developing, seeking the musical element. And this is why the fine arts are more or less assuming musical form also. Music is humanity's artistic future, and can also come to expression in the dramatic arts. The Goetheanum building in Dornach was musically structured, which is why its architecture, sculptural forms and paintings were so little understood originally. The new building currently being planned will also meet with little understanding for this reason, since the musical element must here again be guided into sculpture and painting and their interplay in a way that accords with humanity's evolution.

But something of the most sublime nature, the approach of the figure of Christ—indeed, the living, spiritually living figure of Christ—has been portrayed in a wonderful way in painting, during the Renaissance and in art that preceded it; yet in future this must be found through the musical element. You see, the urge to do this was there—was present in Richard Wagner, and ultimately he introduced it into his *Parsifal*. But his *Parsifal* only offers a hovering, symbolic hint of the influx of the Christ impulse into the physical, sensory world, where this impulse seeks to invoke its most Christian element—the dove appears and so forth. Communion is represented symbolically. Wagner does not achieve in music what really intrinsically embodies the Christ impulse in the cosmos and in the realm of earth. But music will be capable of offering this Christ impulse to the world in tones, in configured tones, in soul-imbued, spirit-imbued tones. Where music is inspired by anthroposophic spiritual science it will find the ways to do this, for it will discover how to enliven the Christ impulse alive in the cosmic and telluric realms, embodying it as symphonies of tones, in a purely artistic and soulful way.

To undertake this we need only have the capacity to deepen our experience of the major thirds with something approaching an inward mystical sensibility. We must experience this as something that is musically very inwardly contained in us. We must try to sense the realm of the fifths as something that has an encompassing, enveloping gesture, a quality, as we grow into the configuring of fifths, of reaching the boundaries between the human and the cosmos, where the cosmos resounds into the human, the human yearns outwards into the cosmos, and even in its yearning grows stormy and turbulent. Then, through the mystery that unfolds between the realm of the major thirds and the fifths, we can experience something of what seeks its way out into the cosmos from our human interiority. And if we then succeed in first allowing the life of the cosmos to sound forth in the dissonances of sevenths, where these dissonances utter what we can feelingly experience in the cosmos as we make our way out into the diverse regions of the spirit, and if we let these seventh dissonances slowly fade so that, as they do so, they acquire a particular quality, then, in their slow fading, they gain something that embodies the way a musical firmament presents itself to musical sensibility.

And then, having previously already intimated a subtle minor experience within the major experience, we can find in this hovering and gradual fading of the seventh dissonances, in this self-configuring of the seventh dissonances into a totality that becomes almost harmonious, almost consonant because it is fading, the possibility, in an intense minor quality, of drawing from the dissonances of the seventh, from their almost harmonious fading, the path back into the realm of the minor fifths, and from there can infuse the region of fifths with that of the minor thirds. If one can do this one engenders a musical experience of incarnation, and specifically of the incarnation of Christ.

You see, we can feel our way out into what is, for cosmic sensibility, only an apparently dissonant realm of the sevenths that we configure into a firmament through having the octave as it were behind it, although only approximately so; and by encompassing this in our feeling, we can then take the path back as I suggested and discover that the seed form of the consonance of the minor thirds offers a possibility for representing the incarnation in musical terms. And then, as we make our way back to the major mode in this realm, the clarion call of Christ's 'hallelujah' can ring out in a purely musical way through the tonal configurations. By configuring music in this way we can conjure forth an immediately supersensible experience and make it available to musical sensibility.

The Christ impulse can be found in the realm of music. And the dissolution of the symphonic mode into something no longer entirely musical—as we find this in Beethoven—can be led back again into the truly cosmic sway of the musical element. Bruckner attempted this, though with a certain narrowness and, let's say, within certain traditional constraints. We can see how he reached this point but got no further if we study his posthumous symphony. On the one hand it is a wonderful work; on the other we see how he is feeling his way forwards through intrinsically musical elements but failing to arrive at a full experience of them since one can only encompass them in the way I suggested, progressing within a purely musical mode and finding there the essence, the core experience that can conjure a tonal world.

As long as humanity does not succumb to decadence, anthroposophic Inspiration will certainly eventually give rise to what I have indicated here. It depends on people themselves but it will be possible for the true form of the Christ impulse to be made outwardly manifest in music.[40]

4. THE INTERVALS AS FUNDAMENTAL MUSICAL PHENOMENA AND HUMAN EVOLUTION AS REFLECTED IN OUR EXPERIENCE OF THEM

Rudolf Steiner described the evolution of the cosmos, the earth and the human being, and the phases of human biography too, in terms of cycles of seven developmental stages. Thus the seven basic musical intervals from the prime through to the seventh are also the qualitative expression of unfolding development. During the Munich Congress in 1907, and then again in the First Goetheanum, Steiner made this 'spiritual music' of the intervals visible in the sculptural forms of the seven capitals and their motifs.

The capitals of these columns represent [. . .] experiences of the 'seer' (though this is no longer a fitting name here) in the world of spirit. This involves perceiving the primal powers that consist of spiritual tones. The sculptural forms of the capitals are translations of what the 'seer' hears. They are in no way arbitrary but arise quite naturally when the clairvoyant allows the spiritual music of the harmony of the spheres to stream through his whole being and then guide his shaping hand. The sculptural forms here are really a kind of 'frozen music' that gives expression to cosmic secrets. It will appear self-evident to someone who understands what is at work here that these shapes assume the form of column capitals. The foundation of the physical evolution of earthly beings lies in the world of spirit, which sustains it. Now all evolution depends on progress through seven stages. (We should not regard the number seven here as a kind of 'superstition' but as the expression of a spiritual law, in the same way that the seven colours of the rainbow are the expression of a physical one.) The earth itself is evolving through seven conditions, each of which is given the name of one of the seven planets, thus Saturn, Sun, Moon, Mars, Mercury, Jupiter and Venus conditions. [. . .] But it is not just a planet that evolves in this way. *Every* process of evolution passes through seven stages, and, in modern spiritual science, each stage bears a planetary name. In this way the forms of the pillar capitals represent the spiritual supports of these changing conditions. But we fail to understand what is involved here if we interpret the forms in a merely rational way. We have to gaze upon them with an artistic sensibility, live our way into them, and allow their forms to affect us. Without seeing this, people will think they have only allegories, or at most symbols, in front of them.[41]

On 1 January 1915, Steiner described to artists and colleagues working on the Goetheanum building how the intervals, illustrated by the sequence from prime to fifth, can in a sense be windows through which the soul enters the world of spirit.

We can discern a time approaching when we will fully immerse ourselves in the feelings that can arise for us from the spiritual-scientific world-view, a time when the path towards art and artistic practice will change in many respects from what it once was. It will become much more vital. The human soul will gain a far more intense experience of the means of artistic creativity than has been true in the past. The soul will be far more intimately imbued by colour and tone, having in a sense a moral, spiritual experience of them so that what the artist creates can appear before us as the traces of his experiences in the cosmos.

In the past era, the stance of artists and those who enjoyed their art was, largely, a kind of outward appeal to what can come towards the artist from without. Dependency on outward perception of nature and a 'model' grew ever more pronounced. I am by no means suggesting that the art of the future should one-sidedly further a departure from nature or outward reality. Not at all. But rather we need to commune with the outer world still more intensively, going beyond merely outward impressions of colour, tone and form, and reaching to what we can experience behind these phenomena, what comes to expression in colour, tone and form.

Human souls will make remarkable discoveries in future in this respect. They will really unite their moral, spiritual being with what sensory appearance conveys to us. In this realm we can look forward to an infinite deepening of the human soul.

[...]

In a very similar way human soul life will be deepened and enlivened through the world of tone. In the past people experienced a tone as such and then the relationships between one tone and others. In future, people will be able to experience what underlies a tone, what lies behind it. They will if you like regard the tone as a window through which they enter the world of spirit; and then how one tone relates to another, follows or precedes it in melodies, will not be dictated by vague feelings but instead the soul will have distinct moral, spiritual experiences underlying each tone. The soul will experience this realm through tones. As if through a window the soul will penetrate the world of spirit. In experiencing each tone, its secrets will be revealed behind it.

As yet we are far from such an experience, we are far from feeling that each tone is a window through which we can emerge from the sensory world into the world of spirit. But this will come. We will experience the tone as an opening that the gods have made from the world of spirit that lies beyond us into this physical, sensory world. Through the tone we will climb from this physical world into the spiritual world. For example, in a prime, experienced in its absolute, intrinsic nature rather than by reference to preceding tones in the scale, we will sense how we ascend from the sensory world into the spiritual world, but do so in a dangerous way. The danger is that, in the prime, penetration of the spiritual realm will threaten to imprison us entirely, acting as a terrible power of suction to fetch us through the window of the tone, so that we vanish completely in the world of spirit. Thus when we experience the prime as an absolute in this way we will sense how we are as yet too spiritually weak in the physical, sensory world, and that we can be sucked up by the spiritual world if we ascend through this window. That will be our moral experience of rising into the spiritual world through the prime. But I am putting this very simply; in fact the experience will be very differentiated and include the sense of infinitely diverse details.

And when we rise from the physical into the spiritual world through the window of the second, we will feel as if there are powers in the spiritual world that, if you like, have mercy on our weakness, who say: 'Well, you were weak in the physical, sensory world! If you rise up from it only through the prime then I must dissolve you, suck you up, fragment or crush you. But if you rise here through the second I will bring towards you something from the world of spirit, and remind you of something that also exists there.'

It is remarkable: when we rise into the spiritual world from the physical through the second, it is as if a sum of tones, a number of tones resound towards us and receive us. By contrast it seems as if we enter an entirely silent world when we penetrate the world of spirit through the prime. Rising through the second, we enter a world in which different high tones resonate, all slightly different, and seek to console us for our weakness. But this entry occurs in a way that of course must not be done if we were to enter a physical house through the window and took the whole window with us as we did so. The owner would be startled if we entered through the window and brought the whole window inside with us. But in the world of spirit that is exactly what must be done—we must bring the tones with us and identify with them, live fully with them in the world of spirit beyond the thin skin that separates us from the rest of our physical surroundings.

When we enter the world of spirit through the interval of the third, we will still retain a great or even greater weakness. Entering through this window we will feel that we were very weak in the physical, sensory world in relation to its spiritual content. But through the third—for at this point we ourselves have become tone, we ourselves are the third—we will feel that in that further realm we have friends who, though not a third themselves, approach us according to how we were constituted in the physical sense world. Whereas entering the world of spirit through the second is like the quiet resonance of many tones in which we live in a generalized way, entering through the third will bring towards us friendly tones, as it were. Those who wish to become composers will have to penetrate the world of spirit through the third especially, for it is here that the tone sequences, tone compositions will arise that stimulate their artistic creativity. It is not always the same 'tone friends' whom one will meet here; their nature will depend on how, when we enter the life of spirit through the third, we have been in our whole life, in our mood, experience, temperament. An infinite multiplicity of tonality will arise here.

If we enter the world of spirit through the fourth, we will have a curious experience: that now tones surface yet come from no direction, but that what has already emerged, the experiences we have undergone with the third, live in the soul in memories that flow freely. And we will find, having entered the world of spirit through the fourth, as we continue to live thus with our tone memories, that they continually assume new colourations: sometimes the brightest luminosity and cheerfulness, while at other moments they grow subdued in the most abject sorrow; sometimes sunny and light, then sunk in mournful gloom, and as quiet as the grave. The tempering of the voice, the rising and sinking of the tone, in brief the unfolding moods of a tonal work, will arise in this passage through tone memories.

The fifth will give rise to more subjective experiences, and will exert a stimulating, enriching effect on our inner experience. It will in a sense act like a magic wand that conjures forth the secrets of the tone world from immeasurable depths.

We will have such experiences when we do not merely look upon the world's phenomena, or listen to them, but instead inwardly experience them. This kind of experience, especially through colours and tones but also in forms or in any artistic medium, is the path we must seek, that humanity must pursue in order to get beyond a merely outward stance towards things and the processes at work in them—the characteristic of a materialistic age. Instead we must seek to plumb the depths of things, to enter their secrets.

If this happens then awareness will dawn in people—and this is of huge significance—of their connection with divine-spiritual powers that remain subconscious for materialistic consciousness, powers that lead and guide us through the world. And then, above all, something like an inward experience will arise of powers which, for instance, guide us onwards from one incarnation to the next.

If we do not heat a train engine it cannot pull the carriages. We continually have to kindle and fuel the powers that bring about what happens in the world. Similarly, we have to kindle the powers which move us forward. And this does happen. But we must learn to know that we are connected with these powers.[42]

Especially in his lectures on tone eurythmy, Rudolf Steiner focused on the intervals as fundamental elements of music. Below we reproduce a few striking passages from the so-called Tone Eurythmy Course (GA 278) that relate to diverse intervals and the experiential qualities they elicit. Firstly, on 20 February 1924, he said:

And in a time like this, if music is also to become gesture, if the experience of music is to become gesture, we have to point to musical experience as such, to the fact that the third embodies inwardness, the fifth conclusion, and the seventh an emergence from oneself. [. . .] With the third we are intimately at home with ourselves. With the fifth we arrive at the boundaries of our body. The fourth lies between them. And the fourth has this magnificent and remarkable quality that we experience ourselves inwardly but not in such an intimate way as we do in the third. But nor do we as yet reach our boundary, the surface of our skin. We experience ourselves in the fourth as being below our surface, a little way below it within ourselves. We are separate from our surroundings, creating ourselves within. It is not like the fifth experience where the outer world takes a compelling hand in our form but in the fourth we still form ourselves according to our own inner needs. The experience of the fourth is actually the realm where we feel ourselves human through our own inner power, whereas in the experience of the fifth we feel ourselves to be human by virtue of the world.[43]

Then, on 25 February, came this:

In musical terms the second is something that does not as yet fully give the musical element but initiates it. It stands at the door of music and questions it.[44]

On 7 and 8 March 1923, Rudolf Steiner gave two lectures on 'The Human Being's Experience of Tone' to the faculty of teachers at the Waldorf school in Stuttgart and the students of the eurythmy school there. As he stressed at the beginning of these comments, he was offering only very fragmentary reflections on this theme. In the first of the lectures he described our experience of the intervals as an expression of the respective stages of evolution of consciousness as human beings gradually woke up to the outer world in sensory life, at the same time experiencing a twilight of their awareness of the divine, spiritual world.

In Atlantean times, the seventh was the core musical experience. If you were to return to these times, you would find that music then bore very little resemblance to music today, and that everything was tuned in recurring sevenths. Not even the fifths were known. And this seventh experience, this musical experience consisting entirely of progressions through the octaves founded on the seventh was one in which people felt themselves completely removed from the earth, released from all earthly bonds. They felt themselves immediately to be in another world. For someone living in those times the experience of music was identical with feeling oneself to be in a world of spirit. This was the paramount experience mediated by the seventh. This continued into post-Atlantean times and played a major part in music until people began to feel averse to the experience. As the human being sought to plumb his physical body, take possession of it, the experience of the seventh started to be felt as painful, mildly painful. And the human being began to find greater pleasure in the experience of the fifth, giving rise to a scale in a sequence like ours that existed for long periods of the post-Atlantean period: d, e, g, a, b and then d, e again. No f or c. In other words we must think away the f and c quality if we return to the mood of the early post-Atlantean period. Instead the passage through the various octaves emphasized the fifths.

Over time, therefore, the fifths became a pleasurable musical experience. But all music, devoid of the third and what we call 'c', was still imbued with a degree of reverie. People felt that this music transposed them into a different element, that it lifted them out of themselves [. . .] And in the fourth post-Atlantean period we find a transition emerging towards the experience of the third. This experience is not yet fully there to begin with; the fifth still dominates, as it does in Chinese music to this day. But this transition towards the experience of the third at the same time signifies that people now felt music to be connected to their own physical organism. Only as we came to experience the third could we feel ourselves to be earthly musicians. Previously, in the experience of the fifth, the experience was one of 'the angel in me' starting to be a musician, of 'the Muse speaking in me'. It would have felt wrong to say 'I sing' at that time. People can only say this when the experience of the third arrives—then we can feel ourselves to be a singer. This is because the experience of the third makes our whole musical experience more inward. And this is also why, in the period of music based on the fifth, it was not yet possible to give music a subjective colouring. The subjective aspect prior to the advent of the experience of the third was always really that the subject felt drawn away and lifted into objectivity. Not until the experience of the third developed could subjective experience rest within itself so that people began to connect with music their own sense of destiny, the feelings of their destined, ordinary life. And this is why something arose that had no meaning at all in the period of the fifths: the experience of major and minor, this corporeal embodiment of human subjectivity and an inner life of feeling resulting from it. This begins during the fourth post-Atlantean epoch and is connected with the interval of the third, along with the distinction that arises now between major and minor. We now see inner subjectivity connected with music and people begin to colour or tinge music with this sensibility. Coloratura only begins to emerge at this point. At this period people are alternately within and outside themselves, the soul swinging back and forth between devotion and self-involvement. Because of this the musical element only now approaches us in a corresponding way. We can put it like this: during the fourth post-Atlantean epoch, the experience of the third begins, and at the same time the possibility of expressing major and minor moods in music. This is where we still are basically. But *how* we stand within this is something that can really only be understood if we comprehend the whole human being in a way that goes well beyond ordinary concepts.

People naturally become used to adding further, anthroposophic concepts to the ones they already possess, simply enlarging the latter by saying that the human being also consists of physical body, etheric body, astral body and I. It has to be like this to begin with since people can only change their views by stages. But we must move beyond this, for things are far more complex than people think. If we think of the development of the earthly human being in his embryonic phase we first have his descent from the world of spirit into the physical world, a descent of the I, the spirit, to the astral realm, to the etheric. And as the I enters the astral, and enters the etheric, it can then engage with the physical embryo, developing forces of growth there and so forth. If we consider the human foetus therefore, we find that this is encompassed by physical forces which are themselves influenced in turn by virtue of the I descending through the astral and the etheric into the physical. If we study the grown human being as he lives in the physical world, we find for example that the I works spiritually through his eyes directly upon the physical body, initially overleaping the astral and etheric, although subsequently this is reincorporated within us. We bring the astral and etheric aspect towards it from within us. And so we can say that the I lives within us in two different ways. First it lives in us by virtue of our becoming human beings on the earth; the I descends into the physical world, building us up from below, from the physical, and encompassing the etheric and astral. But then, once we are grown, the I lives in us by affecting us through our senses, or by exercising a governing influence on the astral: it lives in our breathing, exercising influence without the actual I sphere itself; it engages with the head too where the physical body becomes the organ of the I. Only in the movements of our limbs do we have within us the same activity of nature or the world which we had when we were embryos. Everything else is added. When you walk or dance the same activity is at work in you still as when you were embryos. All other activities, especially that of the head, were added as the down-streaming currents fell away.

Now the experience of music passes through us in our entirety, specifically with involvement of what has descended furthest in us and which, therefore, in a sense approached us initially from outside our human nature before we developed as earthly human beings, forming the foundation for embryonic development, and which now lives only in us because we can move, can also move gesturally. This element in us is at the same time the foundation for the lower parts of the octave, thus c, c sharp, d and d sharp. Now this becomes disordered as you can also see on the piano, because of entering the etheric realm. The lowest notes of the octave—any octave—call initially upon what lies in our limb system, and therefore in our most physical aspect. Then, roughly from e onwards in the scale, the etheric body resonates also, continuing to do so through to f, f sharp and g. And then we reach a higher sphere where what works in the vibrations of the astral body is living. And then the whole business culminates. If we start from c and c sharp and arrive at the seventh here, we come to a region where we must stop really. The experience comes to a halt and we need an entirely new element.

If I can put it like this, as we begin the octave we start from our interior I, the physically alive interior I. And then we rise through the etheric body and astral body to the seventh, and must now pass on to the directly experienced I as we reach the octave. We have to find ourselves anew, a second time, when we reach the octave. In a sense we must say that the human being within us lives in all seven tones, but we know nothing of it. This inner human being pushes against us in c, c sharp, then, because it pushes against us from there, shakes and resonates through our etheric and astral body when, let's say, we reach an f or f sharp; the etheric body vibrates and pushes up against the astral body—this originates below in the etheric body—and then we come to the tones up to the seventh, and have the astral experience here. But we are not really aware of all this. We only sense it. But now the octave experience brings us the discovery of our own self at a higher level. The third leads us inwards; the octave leads us to possess ourselves again a second time, to feel ourselves once more.

You have to regard these terms I use as approximations, surrogates only, and keep going back to the actual experiences. And then you can see how the musical experience really seeks to lead us back again to what we lost in primordial times. In very ancient times when the feeling of the seventh composed people's whole experience of the scale, they felt themselves in music to be integrated beings standing upon earth who were lifted out of themselves in the experience of the seventh. In other words, they felt themselves to be in the world. For them, music was the possibility of feeling themselves in the world. Teaching music to people in those days was at the same time religious instruction, for then they understood immediately, through music, that they were not only earthly in nature but also at the same time lifted away from the earth. This became increasingly inward. The experience of the fifth arrived, in which people still felt united with what lived in their breathing. This period of the fifths was in essence the time when people had this feeling. The experience they had, though they could not express it in words, was this: 'I breathe in, I breathe out. I especially feel this experience of the breathing in great fear, when my breathing is modified. But the element of music does not live in me at all, it lives in my inbreathing and outbreathing.' People felt that they continually departed from and then returned to themselves in their experience of music. The fifth encompassed this in- and outbreathing, while the seventh concerned outbreathing alone. The third enables us to experience the inward continuation of our breathing process. For all these reasons you can explain the transition from a pure, accompanied singing as this existed in ancient times of human evolution to singing on one's own. Initially singing developed in response to some outer tone, an outer tone configuration. Singing later emancipated itself from this, and at the same time instrumental playing became separate and distinct too, also emancipated itself.

Now we can say that in his musical experience the human being felt himself to be one with the world. He felt himself to be neither in nor outside himself. He would not have been able to hear a single instrument or a separate, distinct tone in the very earliest times—this would have seemed to him like a lonely ghost. He could only experience a tone composed of both an outward objectivity and inner subjectivity. Thus experience of music can be distinguished according to these two aspects, the objective and subjective.

This whole experience naturally penetrates all music today. On the one hand we have something that gives music a very distinct position, which is that in musical experience we do not yet find a connection with the world. This connection with the world through music will come when the octave experience comes about as I outlined it. Then musical experience will become evidence of the existence of God through the fact that people experience the I twice, first as physical I within, and second as spiritual I without. And when it becomes as common to employ octaves as one does sevenths, fifths and thirds—for as yet they are not used in this way—this will arise as a new way of proving the existence of God. This will be the octave experience. People will say this: 'When I experience my I the first time, in the prime, as it lives on earth, and then experience it again, in the spirit, then this is an inner proof for me of God's existence.' But this will be evidence of a kind different from the Atlantean's seventh-interval experience, where all music was evidence of God's existence. It was not in the least, though, evidence of the existence of one's own being. In growing musical the great spirit possessed you. At the moment you made music, the great spirit was in you. The great progress of humanity in the realm of music will be that one is not only possessed by God but also possesses oneself at the same time; and this will lead to people experiencing the scale as themselves, but their selves as simultaneously in both worlds. You can imagine the huge deepening that music will be able to undergo in future, bringing people not only to the kind of experience they can have through works of music today but one where they can become quite differently constituted while they listen to music, different as human beings. They will feel they have exchanged one existence for another and then feel they have been given back to themselves again. The development of music will lie in this feeling of a far-distant human capacity. And so we can say that the five ancient tones of d, e, g, a and b have been complemented to the very greatest degree by f, but not yet really by c. We still await the time when this really fully assumes its whole significance for human sensibility.[45]

On the second day Rudolf Steiner took up this theme again, and presented reflections on melody, harmony and rhythm, as well as a small digression on music education and the importance of the fifth in the early years.

Yesterday I spoke of the role of the interval of the fifth in musical experience on the one hand, and on the other of the third and the seventh. You probably realized from my account that a progression in fifths is still connected with an experience of music that leads a person to feel drawn out of himself, so entering a kind of reverie, a lifting away from the earth. This becomes more understandable if we consider the seven octaves from the lowest up to C7. Within this range the fifth can appear twelve times; and thus the sequence of seven octaves also conceals a twelvefold scale of fifths.

What does this mean in relation to our whole musical experience? In the experience of fifths, the human being's I is in movement outside of his physical organism. You can say that we progress through the seven octaves in twelve steps and that through this experience of the fifths we are in movement outside our physical organism.

If we now return to our experience of the third—and this is true both of the major and minor third—we come to an inner movement within us. Here the I in a sense is within the confines of the human organism. We experience thirds inwardly. In the transition from a third to a fifth—though there are stages between, but that is of no account here—we experience the transition from inner to outer experience. And so we can say that in the one case, in the experience of the third, we feel a quality of inner consolidation, a perception of being within ourselves, whereas in the experience of the fifth the mood is one of perceiving ourselves within the divine world order. With the fifth we step out into the wide cosmos, and in the third we return to the dwelling of our own organism. Between these two lies the experience of the fourth.

For anyone who wishes to fathom the secrets of music, this experience of the fourth is perhaps one of the most interesting of all. This is not because the experience or mood of the fourth itself is intrinsically the most interesting, but because it stands at a boundary between the fifth as apprehension of the outer world and the third as inward perception. The experience of the fourth lies precisely at the boundary of the human organism. And yet we do not feel the outer, physical world in the fourth but instead the world of spirit. In a sense we look upon ourselves from without, if I can use a visual expression to convey an auditory experience. In the fourth—we are not aware of this, though the feeling we have of it is based on this—we feel ourselves to be amongst the gods. Whereas in the experience of the fifth we must forget ourselves to be amongst gods, we do not need to forget ourselves in the fourth. Here we walk around as a human being in the divine world, if you like. We stand at the very outer edge of our human nature, still possess it, yet look back upon it in a sense from the other side.

The experience of the fifth as spiritual experience faded from humanity. Nowadays we do not have this fifth experience that once existed around 500 BC. In those times, when people experienced the fifth they had the sense of standing in the world of spirit. They needed no instrument to create a fifth but producing a fifth themselves, and still possessing the faculty of Imagination, they felt it to be unfolding in the divine world. They still had the imaginative capacity, in relation to music too. In the experience of the fifth in the realm of music an objectivity still existed. Humanity had lost this objective experience earlier in the case of the fourth. But for a long time later the fourth remained an experience that made people feel they were living and moving in an etheric realm. In the experience of the fourth, if I can put it like this, they felt something like the sacred wind that had brought them into the physical world. It seems very likely from their comments that Ambrosius and Augustine may still have felt this. Then this experience of the fourth was also lost, and an outer instrument was needed to assure an objective experience of the fourth.

Here at the same time we are pointing to the nature of musical experience in very ancient periods of human evolution. Here the human being did not yet have the third, he only descended as far as the fourth [...]. He did not distinguish in the same way as now between 'I sing' and 'there is singing'. The two things were one and the same for him. A person was outside himself when he sang, and at the same time had an external instrument. In a sense he had the impression of a wind instrument or also a stringed instrument, the impression, the imagination of it. Musical instruments first approached humankind as imaginations. They were not invented by trial and error but were drawn from the world of spirit—with the exception of the piano.

Now at the same time we have the origin of the song. Today it is difficult to give a sense of what singing was like in the period when the experience of the fifth was still pure. Singing was still something like faithful expression. People sang but this singing was at the same time a speaking from the world of spirit. People were aware that if you were speaking of cherries and grapes you needed worldly words, but if you were speaking of the gods you needed to sing.

And then came the time when people no longer had imaginations, though still their residue, which, though they do not recognize this today, are the words of language. An embodiment of the spirit in the sung tone led on to embodiment of the words of speech in the sung tone. This is a step into the physical world. And only then was song inwardly emancipated, later, in arias and so forth. That is a later stage.

So if we look back to the primordial singing of humankind, this is a speaking by the gods and a speaking of the workings of the gods. And as I said, the fact of the twelve fifths in the seven octaves shows that the interval of the fifth gave human beings the capacity to move outside themselves through music. They only approach more closely to themselves in music in the fourth.

Yesterday someone quite rightly said that we experience a kind of emptiness in the fifth. Naturally this is so because people no longer have the faculty of Imagination, and the fifth corresponds to an imagination, whereas the third corresponds to an inner perception. Today therefore we experience something empty in the fifth, and have to fill this with the material nature of an instrument. This marks the transition in music from a more spiritual epoch to a later materialistic age.

We must regard the relationship which people had with their musical instruments in ancient times as a unity in the highest degree. The ancient Greek even found it necessary when acting to amplify his voice by means of an instrument. Only later did things become more inward. In ancient times the experience of music was one in which people felt they bore a certain closed circle of tones in them, reaching neither all the way to the lowest tones nor all the way to the highest. They had this sense of being endowed with a narrow sphere of musical experience while the musical realm extended further in both directions in the cosmos. For this, they felt, they needed instruments, so as to enter this cosmic realm of music. And now we have to consider the other elements of music if we wish to acquaint ourselves with this whole relationship.

Today harmony is at the very centre of all musical experience, not just singing or instrumental music. Harmony directly addresses our feelings, and what comes to expression in it is experienced through our feeling. Now feeling is something that occupies the centre of our whole experience as human beings. In one direction it transforms into will and in the other into thinking and picturing. If we study the human being we can say that feeling is in the middle, and in one direction it runs into thinking and in the other into will. Harmony addresses feeling directly and is experienced in feeling. But the human being's whole feeling nature is two-fold, really. We have a feeling that tends more towards thinking, for instance where we feel our thoughts, think feelingly, and a feeling that tends towards the will. In this case when we perform an action we feel whether it pleases or displeases us. So feeling plays more in one or the other direction from the centre.

Now musical experience has this distinctive characteristic: it cannot be drawn up fully into thinking, since music encompassed only by this faculty, by the brain, would cease immediately to be music; and nor may music sink down entirely into the will. It is inconceivable that music itself could become an abstract symbol, nor a direct impulse of will. When you hear the lunch bell ring, you will go to lunch because this sound calls you to the table, but you will not see music as such as an impulse to the will. This shows that just as little as music may be encompassed entirely by thinking so it may not descend entirely into the will either. In both directions it has to be held back. The experience of music must unfold in the realm that lies between thinking and will, must unfold entirely in the part of us that does not actually belong to ordinary daily awareness at all but has something to do with what descends from worlds of spirit, is embodied and passes once more through death. It is subconsciously present in us. This is why music has no direct correlate in external nature. As we find our way into earthly life, we encompass what can be immediately conceived and what we enact as will. But music does not extend as far as thinking and will. Yet the tendency exists for harmony to radiate towards thinking, if you like. It must not enter thinking as such but it shines in its direction. And this emanation towards the realm of our mind, where otherwise we think, is accomplished by melody.

Melody leads music from the realm of feeling into thinking. A melodic theme is not the same thing as thinking, but it does rise towards the realm where thinking otherwise lies. Melody bears a resemblance to thinking but is not thinking; it still very much unfolds in feeling life. The significant thing about melodic experience is that it renders our head available to feeling. Otherwise our head is only open to concepts but through melody it becomes available for feeling, real feeling. Through melody in a sense we push our heart into our head. In melody you become free as you otherwise only do in thinking. Feeling is clarified, purified. Everything outward falls away from it, but at the same time it becomes feeling through and through.

But now in the same way that harmony can tend to rise towards thinking, it can incline downwards towards the will. But it must not arrive there, must catch hold of itself, if you like, in the will realm, and this occurs through rhythm. Melody bears harmony upwards while rhythm bears it towards the will. This gives rise to harnessed will, to will unfolding in a measured way in time; a will that does not act outwards on the world but remains bound to us ourselves. But this is genuine feeling which in this way extends into the realm of the will.

At this point you will find it understandable that a schoolchild more easily finds melodic understanding than an understanding for harmony. This shouldn't be seen pedantically of course. There is never any room for pedantry in art. Naturally you can bring all kinds of things to the child. But in the same way that in the early years the child by his nature only understands fifths, or at most fourths, but not thirds—and inwardly understands the latter only from the age of eight—so we can also say that a child easily understands melody but not harmony until the age of eight or nine. Of course the child understands the tone as such, but cultivating a sense of harmony in music is really only possible from this age onwards. Rhythm however assumes diverse forms. The child will understand a certain inner rhythm from a very early age. But apart from this instinctively experienced rhythm we should not plague a child with rhythm as such, for example in instrumental music, until around the age of eight. At this point we can direct his attention to such things. We can 'read' from the child himself what is needed in music education, and we will find here more or less the same stages that otherwise figure in Waldorf educational practice.

Now if you focus your attention on rhythm you will find that it is what actually triggers or initiates music. This is because it has an affinity with our will nature, and we must after all set our will in motion if we wish to engage in musical experience. The rhythmic element sets music in motion. Now all rhythm, irrespective of the nature of our relationship with it, is founded on the mysterious connection between pulse and breath: 18 breaths a minute to an average of 72 pulse beats a minute. This 1:4 relationship can of course firstly be modified in the most varied ways, and secondly can also be individualized. Every individual has their own feeling of rhythm but, since this is always approximately the same, people understand each other in respect of rhythm. Thus all rhythmic experience is based on the mysterious connection between the breath and the motion of the heart, the circulation of the blood. And so we can say that whereas melody is borne towards the head from the heart through the stream of breath, thus in outward deceleration and inner engendering of quality, rhythm is borne on the waves of blood circulation from the heart to the limbs, where it captures itself as will. In this way also you can see how music really fills our whole being.

Let us picture the whole musically sensible human being to ourselves as a kind of human spirit. In melodic experience you have the head of this spirit, in harmony you have the chest, the mediating centre of this spirit, and in rhythmic experience you have its limbs.

But what does this actually describe? The human etheric body! Simply by characterizing musical experience, if you do so correctly, you then have the human etheric body incarnate before you. It is just that instead of 'head' we say 'melody', instead of rhythmic system, because this is raised up, we say 'harmony', and instead of 'limb system'—here 'metabolism' would be wrong—we say 'rhythm'. We have the whole human being etherically before us. It is nothing other than this. And in the experience of the fourth a person really experiences himself as etheric body, really as etheric body, except that a kind of summation develops here. In the experience of the fourth, melody, harmony and rhythm are all so interwoven that they cannot be separately distinguished. In the fourth we experience the whole human being at his spiritual boundary, the etheric human being.

If music today were not caught up in the materialistic age, and if everything else we experience today did not completely spoil our experience of the intrinsically musical sphere, then music as such—which has, in itself, reached a world-historical culmination—would inevitably lead everyone to be anthroposophists. If we seek to experience music consciously, it *can* only be experienced anthroposophically. You can do nothing other than experience music anthroposophically.

If you take things as they are, for instance, you can ask yourself the following question. If you study old traditions of spiritual life you will find mention made everywhere of the sevenfold human being. This sevenfold human nature is something that theosophy, the theosophical movement, has adopted. When I wrote my book *Theosophy*, I had to speak of ninefold human nature, as a further subdivision of the basic three; and I only arrived at sevenfoldness from this ninefold structure. As you know:

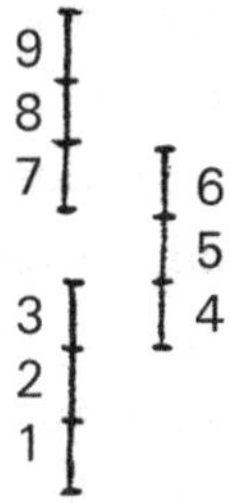

Overlaying of both 6 and 7, and 3 and 4, allowed me to present the sevenfold human being in my book *Theosophy*. But this book could never have been written in the ancient time of the fifths, for back then all spiritual experience arose from having the planetary numbers, the zodiac numbers in the twelve fifths of the seven octaves. The great secret of the human being was there made manifest in the cycle of fifths. In this period of fifths, theosophy could only have taken the form of the sevenfold human being. But my book *Theosophy* was written at a time when the experience of the third is most pronounced, a time therefore of interiority. Here one has to seek the spirit in a way that resembles that in which we descend from the interval of the fifth to that of the third through division. I had to subdivide the separate aspects. And so we can say that the other books which speak of sevenfold human nature originate in the traditions of the ancient period of fifths, the tradition of the cycle of fifths. My *Theosophy* originates at a time when the third plays such an important role in music, a time also in arriving at the third, where things develop so that what is more inward tends towards minor and what is more outward tends towards major; this is why there is unclarity in the superimposition of 3 and 4, thus between the sentient body and the sentient soul. When you say 'sentient soul'—the minor third. When you say 'sentient body'—the major third. Humanity's evolution comes to expression in musical development with far more clarity than in any other domain. But one must relinquish concepts. As I said yesterday, conceptual understanding will not take us there.

And if someone speaks of acoustics, the physics of sound, we get nowhere at all. The physics of tone and acoustics have no significance for any field other than physics. The study of acoustics is not relevant to music itself. To understand the realm of music we have to enter the sphere of spirit.

Now you can see how we have the fourth between the fifth and the third: the fifth so that we feel removed from the earth, whereas with the third we feel that we are in ourselves. With the fourth we are at the boundary between ourselves and the world. Yesterday I told you that the seventh was really the interval of the Atlanteans. They only had sevenths, but they did not have the same feeling we do today. If they became musicians at all they were entirely outside themselves; they were in the great, all-encompassing spirituality of the world, and within absolute movement. They were moved. In the fifth experience movement was still present. The sixth is again between the two. And from this we can see that we experience these three stages, of seventh, sixth and fifth in withdrawal from and hovering above the earth, whereas we enter ourselves in the fourth and with the third are within ourselves. The full musical significance of the octave will only be experienced in future. We have not yet arrived at a heartfelt experience of the second. These things lie in the future. As the human being grows more intensely inward, he will experience the interval of the second and ultimately the single tone as such. I do not know whether any of you will remember that in Dornach once, during a question-and-answer session, I said that the single tone will come to be experienced as something musically differentiated, that in the single tone will lie a whole range of musical differentiation.

If you consider this then you will understand what gives rise to the specific forms of our tone eurythmy. And furthermore, you will understand the instinctual feeling that we should perform the movements for lower parts of the octave, prime, second and third, in a backward direction, whereas we move the upper tones, fifth, sixth and seventh, in a forward direction. These, roughly, would be the forms one

typically makes for this, and that one can use here. And you will gain a sense that these forms are approximately contained in the figures developed for specific pieces of music, that they are present in the experiences of fourth or fifth. It is very necessary that this part here, where the harmony descends through rhythm into the will, comes to particular expression in eurythmy. And so one has the various intervals in the intrinsic forms we make; but also what passes from the intervals into rhythm must be manifest in these forms. And here, quite instinctively, we may perform a smaller movement for the fourth, without actually coming to a standstill—just a small movement. You see, the fourth is actually a kind of real perception, just one from the other side. In a sense, when I say that I'm looking like this with my eyes—I would have to look at the eye itself, the eye would have to gaze backwards, and this would be the experience of the fourth

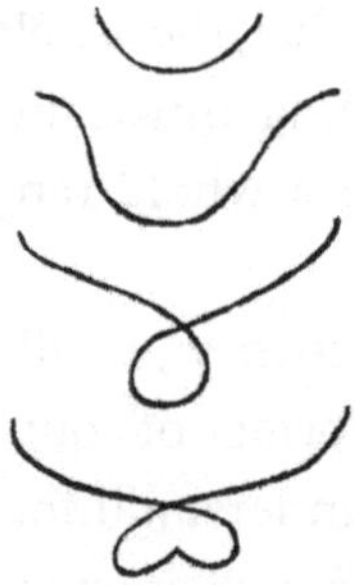

drawn from the soul. The fifth is a true experience of Imagination. If you experience the fifth as you should, you already know subjectively, really, what Imagination is. When you experience sixths you know what Inspiration is. And if you experience sevenths—and survive the experience—you will know what Intuition is. What I mean is that the form of the soul's constitution in the experience of the seventh is the same as that of Intuition in the seer. And the form of soul constitution in the experience of the sixth is the same as the seer's Inspiration. The experience of the fifth is a true experience of Imagination. This state of soul then needs only to be filled with vision, perception, but is certainly already present in the musical realm.

This is why you will frequently hear that in ancient mystery schools, and in the lasting traditions that they gave rise to, clairvoyant perception is also referred to as musical cognition: spiritual-musical cognition. People no longer know why spiritual perception is really musical cognition, a form of perception that lives in the element of music. Actually it would not be so very hard to give the idea of the threefold human being popular currency if people today were conscious of their musical sensibility. Certainly, people have something like a musical sensibility, but they do not stand fully within this as human beings. Really they stand alongside it; in their experience of music, though, something is within their reach. If the experience of music became vivid and vital in people, they would feel that their etheric head lies in melody and the physical has fallen away from it—and this is one aspect of the human being's organization. Then their etheric middle system lies in harmony, the physical likewise falling away from it. Then this is transposed into another octave; and in the system of limbs, again, we have the rhythmic element of music. There is no need to waste too many words on this—it is a tangible experience.[46]

In the next lecture, in the context of another account of musical experience from Atlantean times up to the present, Rudolf Steiner points to the experience of the interval of the ninth in the Lemurian era, before coming full circle by considering music today and in the future.

Thus in this special domain you can see how we can come close to experiencing the cosmos—how the cosmos penetrates us, and how in a sense, when we look back to ancient times, we must seek the most important human experience in the supersensible realm—and then also observe how the time arrives when the human being as sensory, earthly manifestation has to be included in an account of the most important events in the cosmos.

This occurs at the epoch after thoughts have passed from the beings of form to the primal beginnings. And this is expressed in the fact that the ancient era of the fifths—which existed still earlier than this—passes into the age of the thirds, the experience of major and minor.

Now it is especially interesting if we trace this particular experience back to a still more ancient time than the Atlantean, thus back to a period of the human being's evolution on earth that, to our gaze, is a dim and distant, hazy past, though supersensible perception can bring it into clearer focus. Here we look back to an age—you will find this described as the Lemurian age in my *Occult Science*—when the human being cannot as yet be aware of an interval within an octave in musical experience; he perceives an interval instead only in so far as it overreaches the octave, roughly as follows:

c d e f g a h c d

In other words he hears only this interval c–d, that is, the d of the following octave.

In the Lemurian age, we do, certainly, discover human musical experience, but one that cannot unfold through hearing of an interval within an octave. The interval goes beyond the limits of the octave to the first tone of the following one, and from there to the following tone of the octave beyond that. And the nature of this human experience is hard to express in words; but we can perhaps gain a sense of it if I say that a person experiences the second of the next octave and the third of the one after that. He experiences a kind of objective third, and then also the two different thirds, the major and minor. Except that here the third—as he experiences it—is of course not a third as we understand it, which arises only within an octave in relation to the originating prime. In those ancient times a person experienced intervals which we would describe as prime in one octave, second in the next octave, third in a third octave, and in this experience he perceived a kind of objective major and minor, one that was felt to be an expression of the soul experience of the gods. In the Lemurian age, in this distinctive musical experience, people were lifted entirely out of themselves in their perception of these intervals, experiencing the cosmic tones of the gods' jubilation and their cosmic lament. Here we can look back to an age when humankind on earth projected out into the universe what today we experience in major and minor. What we experience inwardly today was projected out instead into the universe in those times. What today swells in our sensibility, our feeling, people in those times heard, when lifted right out of their physical body, as the experience of the gods beyond. Our modern, inner experience of the major mode was heard then in the gods' cosmic jubilation, their jubilance, the expression of their joy at their creation of the universe. And the inner experience of the minor mode as we know it today was something that humankind of the Lemurian era heard as the great lament of the gods at the fact that human beings might succumb to what was recounted in the Bible as the Fall: a lapse from the benevolent divine, spiritual powers.

This is something that resounds for us from that wonderful knowledge of the ancient mysteries, which naturally passed into artistic form. Rather than merely abstract knowledge of the luciferic and ahrimanic temptation and ensnarement which human beings underwent, we can discern that people heard how, in primordial times, the gods made jubilant music in the cosmos in their joy at their creation of the world, and how they prophetically perceived the lapse of humankind from divine, spiritual powers, giving expression to this in their cosmic lament.

This artistic comprehension of something that later assumed ever more intellectual forms sounds forth from the ancient mysteries in a way that deeply and compellingly shows us the one, *single* source from which flowed knowledge, art and religion. And this must persuade us that we should find our way back to the state of soul that will emerge again in inner perception imbued and pervaded by artistic and religious sensibility—a state of soul that once again comprehends in a deep, living way what Goethe meant when he said that beauty is a manifestation of hidden laws of nature which, without it, would have remained forever unknown. The secret of humanity's evolution in earth existence, within earthly growth and development, is revealed to us by this inner unity of all that we must experience through our cognition, religion and art so that, in communion with this world, and in common with it, we can come to our fullest unfolding.

It is true to say that the time has now come when human beings should once more become aware of these things, since otherwise the inner soul quality of human nature must fade and lapse. Today and in the near future, people might well grow arid in soul through a narrowly intellectual life of the mind, grow dull through a narrow form of art, and become generally soulless through a narrow form of religion, if they cannot find the path that leads them to the inner harmony and unity of these three aspects, if they cannot find the way to emerge from themselves more consciously than has previously been the case, and once again perceive and hear the supersensible alongside the sensory realm.

If we draw on spiritual science to look back to the ancient, profound figures of early Greek culture, to individuals whose legacy lived on and was developed in others such as Aeschylus or Heraclitus, we find that these early figures, if they were initiated into the mysteries, all had a similar sense and perception that informed their creative, artistic powers, and which they expressed as Homer did of course—'Sing, O

Muse, of the rage of Achilles, son of Peleus'—not as something that resided within their person but as a power invoked in their religious sensibility in communion with the world of spirit. They had the sense that in primordial times people felt their intrinsic humanity, in their most significant activities—as I related in the case of music, but this was true too of their formulation of thoughts—by emerging from themselves, passing beyond themselves so that their experiences came to them in communion with the gods. The ancient Greeks felt that people had now lost this experience.

This mood of loss of a primordial knowledge and of an innate artistic and religious sensibility certainly weighed heavily on the more profound thinkers of ancient Greece.

Something new must arise today. Modern people must see that by developing the right powers of soul experience they can come to the point of rediscovering what was once lost. We live in the age of the consciousness soul, and we must become conscious that what has become inward in us should find its way outwards again to the divine, spiritual realm. This can happen—and I indicated this in reply to a question that I was asked during the first School of Spiritual Science course at the Goetheanum—and will for instance happen in a particular field, if the inner wealth of feelings experienced in melody can be transferred to the single tone. If, in other words, we not only experience intervals but really also can experience the single tone, in all its inner wealth and multiplicity, as a melody. So far there is scarcely any sense or inkling of this.

But you see how things are progressing: from the seventh to the fifth, from the fifth to the third, from the third down to the prime, and through to the single tone; and then onwards. So that what was once loss of the divine must be transformed in human evolution if humanity is to develop and not go under, must transform again into rediscovery of the divine.

We only properly understand the past if we can balance it with the right picture of our evolution into the future, if we can gain a profound, a shatteringly profound feeling that deeply reflective figures in ancient Greece felt that they had lost the presence of the gods, if we can set against this experience another that rises in our shaken, yet intent and inmost striving: the will to develop the seed spirit within us into flower and fruit so that we can rediscover the gods once more.[47]

5. THE EFFECTS OF MUSIC, AND THE HUMAN EXPERIENCE OF TONE

The human experience of tone is a complex process that for Rudolf Steiner encompasses more than acoustics and neurosensory perception. The soul-spiritual reality of the tone is the foundation for this experience, and—mediated by the vibrations of air—this has a complex connection with etheric and rhythmic processes in us. Steiner here describes from his own clairvoyant enquiries how we experience music. Music's effect on us, both in a potentially negative and positive sense, is then illustrated by general examples.

Our experience of music is based on feeling, but its structure and content, mediated through the ear's auditory perceptions, lives in our thinking. How does this feeling experience arise in music? Our *idea* of tonal configurations, based on auditory and neurosensory processes, does not yet constitute it. Musical experience arises when the breathing rhythm continuing on into the brain encounters what the ear and nervous system accomplish. And the soul does not live merely in what is heard and thought or pictured, but in the rhythm of breathing; the soul experiences what is invoked in the breathing rhythm when nervous system processes impact on this life of rhythm. We just have to see the physiology of the breathing rhythm in the right light, and then we can fully acknowledge that the soul gains this feeling experience through the support of the breathing rhythm in a way that is similar to how it thinks through the support of nerve processes.[48]

If we consider the musical tone itself, the acoustic element is really only the basis, the support, for the tone to manifest in the sensory world. The tone is in fact more than the vibrations of air that reveal it.

We can only understand these things, understand them in our feeling, if we realize that musical experience does not have the relationship with the ear that it is usually assumed to have. Musical experience relates to the whole human being, and the ear has a quite different function in musical experience than we usually imagine. Nothing is more mistaken than to say, 'I hear the tone,' or 'I hear the melody with my ears.' That is simply not true at all. The tone or a melody or any harmony is in fact experienced in our whole being; and this experience comes to awareness through our ears in a very remarkable way. The tones we usually think of are conveyed through the medium of air, aren't they? If we use some instrument other than a wind instrument, the tone still lives in the element of air. But what we experience in the tone has actually nothing to do with air. It's like this: the ear is the organ that in fact separates the airborne aspect from the tone itself, so that we receive the tone we experience as resonance or reflection. The ear is actually the organ that reflects back inside us the tone living in the air, but does so in a way that separates it from the element of air. The tone we hear then lives in the etheric element. Thus the ear is really there, if I can put it like this, to overcome the tone resounding in the air and to reflect the pure etheric experience of the tone into our inner being. The ear is a reflection instrument for our feeling of tone.

We must try to gain a deeper understanding of the whole nature of our human experience of tone. I must repeat that all our ideas and concepts fall into confusion when we seek to understand this. We find it so easy to say that we are a threefold being composed of neurosensory system, rhythmic system, and limbs and metabolism. In all other situations this is all perfectly true, but for our experience of tone, for musical experience, our sense experience is not actually present as it is for other experiences. In musical experience, sensory experience is not present as it is in other perceptions, but is far more interior; and this is because the ear is really the reflecting organ only, and does not connect us with the outer world in the same way as, say, the eye does. Our eyes continually connect us with our outer surroundings in respect of all forms of the visible world, also artistic forms of the visible. A painter uses his eyes, as does anyone who observes nature. But for a musician the ear comes into play only in so far as it is capable of an experience that is distinct from connecting with the outer world in the way that the eye does. The ear is involved in music only by virtue of being a reflecting instrument. And in relation to musical experience we must initially consider the neurosensory system. The ear as direct sensory organ is not part of this, but only mediates inwards. It does not connect us with the external world. Perception of instrumental music is a very complex process, and we will speak of it in due course; but as a sensory organ the ear is not directly involved except in its reflecting capacity.

But when we look further we find that everything connected with our limbs does have a part to play in musical experience, which is why music can easily flow into dance. Our metabolic system however does not play the same kind of role as it does in relation to the rest of the world. When we speak of musical experience therefore, the human configuration is shifted, is called upon differently.

In respect of musical experience we have to say: nerve system, rhythmic system, limb system. Sensory perceptions are concomitant phenomena, not directly involved. They are present because we are sensory beings, and our ears have their importance as sense organs, but not the importance we must ascribe to them in other circumstances. Nor is metabolism present in the same way as usual; it is an accompanying phenomenon. Metabolic phenomena arise but they are of no significance at all. What is important, by contrast, is everything that lives as movement potential in the limbs. This is enormously important for musical experience since we connect dance movements with it. A good part of our experience of music depends on us containing ourselves, holding back the movements. But this in turn will point you to the fact that musical experience is one that encompasses our whole being.[49]

In the experience of tone, in feeling assimilation of music in the soul, the whole human being is always active—the neurosensory system, the rhythmic system and the metabolic-limb system—although only the neurosensory process itself is consciously experienced.

The tone is really something which, we can say, greatly confuses our human outlook. We hear the tone initially as earthly human beings, the air being the medium and bearer of this tone. But that is all it is—the medium. Someone who regards the vibrations of air as the essence of the tone is like someone who says that we only have our physical organism, and there is no such thing as the soul. It is like considering the physical organism only, without finding any inner quality present there. The air's vibrations are only the outer expression of the tone. Its inner essence is largely an etheric element. Our airborne tone originates only from the fact that the air is pervaded by the tone ether, which is the same as the chemical ether. This ether pervades the air and communicates to the air what lives within it, giving rise to what we perceive as tone. This same tone ether, which is at the same time chemical ether—we will speak of all this in more detail on another occasion—chiefly lives in our fluid organism. And so we can distinguish as follows: our own etheric body is living in our fluid organism; from without, though, the tone ether that underlies tone penetrates it from all directions. So please distinguish these things very carefully. We have our etheric body within us, and it works and acts, elaborates thoughts in our fluid organism. But into this fluid organism what we call the chemical ether continually penetrates, enters and departs. If we study the human organism, therefore, we have a complete etheric organism consisting of chemical ether, warmth ether, light ether, life ether and, quite particularly, the chemical ether passing in and out through the body of fluids.[50]

The positive effects of music on the soul can be so great that they fend off and balance out the forces of evil rising within us. This was known in the mysteries in ancient times, and an echo of it lives in Shakespeare,[51] *as Rudolf Steiner shows in a lecture on education.*

If we didn't have music, terrible forces would surface in us. I am utterly sure that traditions from the ancient mysteries were still at work up to the sixteenth and seventeenth centuries, and that there were people up to that point whose spoken and written words were still influenced by these traditions. They no longer fully understood the meaning of this influence, and yet some things that emerge at a relatively late date do quite simply embody memories of ancient mystery knowledge. I have always been deeply moved by these words of Shakespeare: 'The man that hath no music in himself, nor is not moved with concord of sweet sounds, is fit for treasons, stratagems and spoils [...] Let no such man be trusted.' In ancient mystery schools pupils were taught that 'treasons, stratagems and spoils' attack us from within and must continually be fended off, suppressed, and that music counteracts this within us. Music is the means to fend off luciferic powers that rise up within us as 'treasons, stratagems and spoils'. We are all capable of terrible deeds, and it is not without reason, and not for our pleasure only, that we have the element of speech and music in us. This makes us human. Naturally we must remember that the old mystery teachers spoke in a somewhat different vein, in more tangible ways. Instead of 'treasons, stratagems and spoils' as Shakespeare has it, they would have said 'snake, wolf and fox'. The snake, the wolf and the fox are warded off from our inner nature and kept at bay by the element of music. Teachers in the ancient mysteries would always have invoked animal forms to describe what rises up within us and what must be transformed into human qualities. And we can develop real pedagogical enthusiasm when we see the treacherous snake rising from the child and can combat it through speech and music; and likewise the murderous wolf and the spiteful fox or cat. This can imbue us with the right, rational enthusiasm, rather than the burning, luciferic enthusiasm which is the only kind people acknowledge today. So we can recognize this: attack and defence.[52]

The following aphoristic hint by Steiner can make us pause for thought. He draws our attention here to a realm we usually overlook. Concert performances—depending on the spiritually positive or negative content of the music—attract corresponding positive or negative beings.

Then there are spirit beings whose lowest level is the astral body, and who are therefore composed of still finer substance. These beings find the opportunity to join with human beings in the arts expressed in a mobile, moving form, in music. A room that is filled with the sounds of music is an opportunity for these spiritual beings to enter with their astral body as lowest member. A room pervaded by musical tones is certainly a place where the human being creates an interplay between himself and other spirit beings. Through sublime, significant music, a person draws good beings into his sphere; but it is equally true that abhorrent music brings negative astral beings within the human compass. You would find it rather unedifying if I were to describe the ugly, astral forms that dance about when the orchestra plays various modern works. These things are to be taken seriously!

In this way we have seen how our visible world interacts with an invisible world of spiritual beings who stand behind it.[53]

Rudolf Steiner refers to the far-reaching and profound influence of music when he speaks of Apollo, one of the twelve bodhisattvas, who as Orpheus attained the illumination of Buddha status. In certain regions of Europe, the musical education founded on the Orphic tradition prepared the capacity of logical thinking in the fifth cultural epoch.

And thus another teacher of humanity was needed—someone with quite different capacities, who brought down quite different streams of spiritual life from the higher spiritual realms into this world. This other individuality had the task of introducing what has now gradually become apparent in humanity as, primarily, the capacity of logical thinking. There had to be a teacher who bore down to earth something that involves expressing oneself in the forms of logical thinking. This, you see, only developed over the course of time.

What the Buddha accomplished had to be integrated into the rational or mind soul. By virtue of standing midway between the sentient soul and the consciousness soul, this rational sensibility is one that, very distinctively, does not recur, is not recapitulated. The ancient Indian era will recur in the seventh epoch, the ancient Persian in the sixth, while the fourth exists on its own as pivotal period. Similarly, the rational soul exists on its own terms. Though the powers of our intellectual capacity could not be developed in the rational or mind soul and were only to emerge later in the consciousness soul, they had to be prepared and stimulated at an earlier stage. In other words, the impulse for logical thinking had to be given earlier, at the time when the Buddha gave the impulse for conscience. The fourth epoch was one that saw the arrival of conscience and its integration into people's organization. Pure, conscious thinking was to emerge in the fifth epoch with the consciousness soul, but in the third epoch the seed of what is now flowering had to be sown. For this reason, that other great teacher had the task of instilling into the sentient soul the powers that are now apparent as logical thinking. And therefore it is easy to imagine that this teacher was set apart from ordinary human beings to a still greater degree than was the Buddha. In the sentient soul something was to be instilled that was not yet present, really, in any human being of the time. Concepts as these later developed were quite alien to people at the time.

Thus this individuality had the task of sowing the seed for certain powers to grow, although he himself might not or could not employ these powers himself. He therefore had to use quite different powers.

This morning, in my second lecture on 'Anthroposophy', I explained that in the act of seeing in the sentient soul, for example, powers are at work that only really become conscious at a higher level, appearing then as those of thinking. If a great teacher of this kind succeeded in stimulating the sentient soul so that the powers of thinking could penetrate it—as thinking life does unconsciously in the act of seeing, without a person being aware of this—then these powers could be used later at a higher level. This was only possible by a single means. To stimulate the sentient soul in this way, to instill the thinking element into it, this individuality had to act at the time in a very distinctive way: he had to teach not in concepts but through music. Music offers powers which initiate in the sentient soul something which, when it rises into consciousness and is assimilated by it, becomes logical thinking. Thus a mighty being taught through the influence of this distinctive kind of music.

You will think this odd, and perhaps not believe such a thing is possible. And yet this is what happened. In Europe, before Graeco-Roman times, ancient peoples who had not developed qualities that did by contrast evolve strongly in the Orient, had little capacity to think; and this was because they were meant to evolve in a very different way. They had very few of the powers of the rational or mind soul. But instead their sentient souls were more receptive for what emerged from the impulses of a distinctive kind of music, which was really rather different from the music we know today. In Europe we find a time, therefore, when an ancient culture existed that we can call 'musical'. In later, decadent periods, 'bards' became the teachers. But before this, all Europe was filled with an enchanting kind of music. During the third cultural epoch a profoundly musical culture existed in Europe; and the sensibility of people who were quietly awaiting their future destiny was especially receptive to such musical influences. These influences upon the sentient soul resembled the way thinking substance acts in the sentient soul when we see. An influence worked upon the sentient soul, in which consciousness was to arise and appear at a higher level as logical thinking in the consciousness soul. But now, you see, all consciousness, and likewise music and song, comes from the region of light. And this is why music acting on the physical plane gave the sentient soul the subconscious feeling that this music came from regions whence light originates: music and song from the realms of light!

In European regions there was a very ancient teacher—an ancient bard in this sense, the instigator of all bardic culture. He taught through music on the physical plane. And the influences emanating from him communicated to the sentient soul something that resembled a sun dawning, rising and shining. The Greeks encapsulated outer traditions regarding this great teacher in their views of Apollo—a sun god and at the same time the god of music. This Apollo influence came from the West, though another influence upon them also came from the East. The figure of Apollo points us back to this great teacher of early times, who implanted in the human soul the capacity that today emerges as logical thinking.

And a pupil of this great teacher of humanity was likewise named by the Greeks: someone who, however, became his pupil in a very singular way. How was it possible to become this being's pupil? It occurred as follows.

In times when this teacher-being was to influence humankind in the way described, he was not subsumed in the human physical organism but was more than this—more than what walked about as physical human being on the earth. Someone with an ordinary sentient soul was able to receive these musical influences but could not have caused them. A higher individuality had descended, and what lived outwardly was like an appearance or manifestation of him.

But in the fourth post-Atlantean cultural epoch, the Graeco-Roman, it was necessary for this individuality to descend once again, as it were to descend as far as the human level, and to use all the capacities innate in human beings. Yet despite using all these capacities, he was not able to descend fully, since to bring about what I have just described, this pivotal effect, he required capacities whose degree exceeded that of a human organization in the fourth post-Atlantean epoch. What exists in the consciousness soul was already contained in the musical influences and effects; but this could not yet be fully incarnated at that time since it would only be commensurate with the mind soul. And so this individuality, despite his embodiment in a human form and figure, had to hold something back. In the fourth cultural epoch he had to be incarnated in a way that did fill him entirely; but over and above this, the living person possessed something which in a sense extended beyond him. He knew something of the world of spirit that he could not actually employ. He possessed a soul that extended beyond his body.

If we consider this in human terms, there is something tragic about it: that the individuality who had worked as a great teacher in the third cultural epoch had to be re-embodied in a form and figure whose soul extended beyond him, and that this soul capacity could not be used or realized since it exceeded the ordinary scope. This kind of embodiment is called a 'son of Apollo' since what had formerly existed could not be directly embodied, could be incarnated only in a very complex way. In this sense, he was a 'son' who bore in his soul something that in mysticism is usually symbolized as feminine. But this was present in him in a way he could not fully possess since it dwelt in a different world. He bore within him his own feminine soul quality but in a different world to which he had no access. He longed to reach this world, since a part of his self was contained there. This inner tragedy of the reincarnated individuality of the great teacher of former times found its way into Greek myth in a wonderful way, in the name that it gave to the reincarnated Apollo, the 'son of Apollo', which was that of Orpheus.

In the myth of Orpheus and Eurydice we find a wonderful account of the tragedy of this soul. Eurydice is snatched away from Orpheus prematurely and must dwell in a different world. Orpheus descends into the realm of the shades. He still has the capacity to stir and move the beings in the underworld with his music. He is permitted to take Eurydice back with him, but he must not look back, for to look back upon what he once was, and what he cannot now assimilate into himself, will inwardly deaden him or at least expose him to the loss of this aspect.

Thus, in Apollo who becomes Orpheus, we also have a kind of descent of a Bodhisattva—if we wish to use an oriental name—who becomes a Buddha. In the same way we could cite a series of such beings existing through the ages as humanity's great teachers, who, in their deepest descent, when they achieve Buddha-hood, experience something very particular. The Buddha experiences the bliss of inspiring all humanity. The Bodhisattva whom tradition enshrined outwardly in the name 'Apollo' experiences something individual. It was his task to prepare individuality, the quality of I-hood. He experiences the tragedy of the I: that it is not entirely encompassed within itself, the condition also of human beings today as regards this human attribute. The human being strives upwards to the higher I; and this was prefigured in this Greek Buddha or Bodhisattva individuality named Orpheus.[54]

How does the 'seer' experience music in the state of clairvoyance, as opposed to the way we ordinarily experience music? Rudolf Steiner describes this in what follows, and also connects the human and cosmic process of breathing in relation to music.

The seer feels a quite different affinity [. . .] with the art of music. Especially in relation to music it is interesting that the seer experiences things differently when he enters clairvoyantly into the realm of art. Here I must note something that refers to clairvoyance—that this is not an invariable perception but something that arises only in the moments when one places oneself into this state. Thus what I will describe is not an experience of music that occurs except when one intends it. At other times the seer experiences music like anyone else does; and he can compare this with his musical experience in the clairvoyant state. The seer is aware that in this condition he is experiencing music as something entirely inward, and that this tangible quality of soul feels one with the musical element. In the past I have said that the seer develops a new pictorial thinking capacity, conceiving things in a way that gives him a sense of being at home in creative architectural and sculptural work. By grasping things not only through thinking but at the same time developing feeling and shaping powers, and in a way that connects these with each other, the division between feeling and will is overcome. In the seer we must speak of a feeling will and a will-imbued feeling; a soul experience connects these two, which in ordinary awareness run parallel to each other, into a totality of feeling will. This feeling will can have either a stronger will or feeling nuance. Now when the seer engages with music in a soul condition that is elevated towards the world of spirit, he experiences as authentically musical, genuinely musical, everything arising in his soul as feeling nuance. Here one does not separate the objective tone from the subjective tone experience. In the seer's experience these are one, so that the soul streams in the same way as the tones stream into each other, except that everything is spiritualized. In this experience, the soul is poured out into the musical element so that one knows that what is experienced through this newly developed feeling will comes from the same source as that which the composer has infused into his tones. Precisely in music it is interesting to study how the creative musician draws on the unconscious to invoke a spiritual reality perceived by the seer, and infuse his work with it. In music we have the manifestation of this underlying reality.

In a quite different way, the wonderful structure of our organism plays a part in all unconscious factors unfolding in our soul life. It is increasingly apparent that our organism cannot be regarded as ordinary biology and physiology describes it, but that it must instead be seen as a reflection of a spiritual archetype. What we bear within us is the reflection of a spiritual archetype. Through birth or conception, we enter existence, using the laws of heredity but also what descends from a world of spirit, of which the physical is a reflection. There is no time today to detail how this happens. But it is an objective fact that the activity in our organism unfolds in accordance with laws that reflect the spirit. This is particularly noteworthy in music. We think that the ear is involved in our enjoyment of music, and perhaps our brain's nervous system, but that is only a very external view. In this realm physiological understanding is still in its infancy, and will only come to more maturity when artistic thoughts inform the fields of physiology and biology. Our experience of music depends on something quite different from merely auditory processes or what occurs in our brain's nervous system. We can describe it like this. Whenever we breathe out, breathing causes the cerebrospinal fluid in the brain, the interior of the head, to descend through the spinal column to the diaphragm area. When we breathe in, the reverse occurs: the cerebrospinal fluid is pushed upwards towards the brain. Thus a continual rhythmic rising and falling of the cerebrospinal fluid occurs. If this were not so, the brain would not be buoyed up sufficiently to prevent the blood vessels below it being crushed. The fluid prevents the weight of the brain from crushing them. This cerebrospinal fluid rises and falls in the arachnoidal cavity, in both more and less elastic vessels; and as it rises and falls in and out of less elastic vessels, flowing through channels of varying extension, this gives rise to a wonderful rhythmic activity. The whole human organism, apart from the head and the limbs, comes to expression in this inner rhythm. What streams in through the ear as tone, lives in us as tone idea or picture, becomes music as it meets the inner music that comes about because our whole organism is a remarkable musical instrument.

One can cite some pretty unsubtle facts to show that we are constructed according to a remarkable cosmic lawfulness.

Most trivially, we breathe approximately 18 times a minute. If we calculate how many times this is in a day of 24 hours, we come to 25,920 breaths. Then, if we calculate the age we live to, roughly, we can settle on 'three score years and ten'—70 or 71, although of course many live longer than that. If we work out how many 24-hour days there are in this number of years, we find it is 25,920—equal to the number of breaths you take in a day! The world breathes us out and in again; we are born and die. In this lifetime, a 'human day', the world takes the same number of breaths (days) that we take in 24 hours.

Now consider the Platonic year: the sun rises in a particular zodiac sign and the spring equinox point keeps moving onward. In ancient times the sun rose at the vernal equinox in the sign of Taurus, then in Aries, and now in Pisces. Modern astronomy is a schematic business. This point of the spring equinox seemingly—and only seemingly, but this does not matter—passes round the whole circle of the heavens and eventually returns to its starting point again after a very great number of years, in fact after 25,920 years. The Platonic year is 25,920 years! Now take a person who is 71 years old: he has seen 25,920 days go by. And take a single human day of 24 hours: 25,920 breaths. And so we are integrated into the rhythm of the cosmos. There are many similar reflections we could pursue, and I believe that no abstract religious ideas could invoke such a sense of reverence as this awareness that we ourselves, our outward physical organisms, are embedded in this way in the macrocosm, in the cosmic order. The seer tries to spiritually penetrate this affinity with the cosmos, which comes to expression in our inner music. What emerges here from the organism, what rises up in the soul—the soul's harmony and concord with the cosmos—is the unconscious element of artistic creation. The whole world resonates with us when we are really artistically creative.

Here you have the common source of art and seership: unconscious in the artist as he infuses cosmic laws into substance; conscious in the seer as he seeks to perceive what is purely spiritual through his visionary consciousness.[55]

6. RUDOLF STEINER ON GOETHE AND SCHOPENHAUER, AND THEIR VIEW OF MUSIC

In his studies of music, Steiner refers repeatedly to both Goethe and Schopenhauer. Goethe he sees as 'the father of a new aesthetics', upon whom Steiner's own aesthetics were founded. In a lecture in Vienna in 1888, he speaks briefly of Goethe and music. Then in Weimar, when he was editing Goethe's scientific writings, he reorganized the latter's Proverbs in Prose,[56] *which contains the following key sentences on music.*

The content of beauty, the substance or matter underlying it, is therefore always something real, has direct reality, and the form of its appearance is an ideal one. Here we see the truth to be the very reverse of what German aesthetics asserts, for it has simply turned things upside down. Beauty is not the divine in the garb of sensory reality; no, it is sensory reality in a divine garb. The artist does not bring the divine to earth by allowing it to flow into the world, but rather by raising the world into the sphere of the divine. Beauty is appearance because it conjures before our sensory perception a reality which inherently represents an ideal world. 'More than on *what*, reflect on *how*.' *How* something comes to expression is the important thing. The 'what', the content, remains a sensory reality, but the manner in which it appears, the form, becomes ideal. Where this ideal manifestation appears best in the sensory world here we also find the highest art. Goethe says of this: 'The grandeur of art appears perhaps in music in its most eminent form since it has no substance from which it must be distilled. It is entirely form and content in one, and gives sublimity to everything it expresses.' We do not yet have an aesthetics founded on the definition that 'beauty is a sensory reality that appears as if it were idea'. This must still come. We can sum it up as 'the aesthetics of the Goethean world-view'. And this is the aesthetics of the future.[57]

In the same volume, V, Goethe's fragment on a theory of music was first published, with a brief commentary by Steiner.[58]

'Music is sacred or profane. When sacred, it is entirely worthy of itself, and here it has the greatest influence upon life, retaining this through all times and eras. When profane it should above all be cheerful.'[59]

'A music that confuses the sacred and profane character is godless, and where, in its indeterminacy, it takes pleasure in expressing weak, pitiful, abject feelings, is tasteless. It is not serious enough to be sacred, and yet lacks the chief character of its opposite, which is gaiety.'[60]

'The sacred nature of church music and the jocular and playful nature of folk melodies are the two lynchpins of true music. In these two realms it always exerts an inevitable effect: either reverence or dance. To confuse the two is error, this dilution becomes insipid; and if music turns to didactic poems or descriptive ones and suchlike, it grows cold.'[61]

Steiner remarks as follows on these 'proverbs in prose', at the same time expressing his own view of music.

Music has no models in reality (finding no material there). The musician creates form and content from within. This is why, of all the arts, music will be least susceptible to seeking content, the *what,* in the outer world, instead of the *how,* which is the form created by the artist. For this reason music is best fitted to raise itself above reality and guide us towards the deeper aspects of life, yet at the same time also to allow us to forget reality.[62]

Around 23 years after Goethe's scientific writings were published, Steiner spoke about Goethe's theory of music at the first anthroposophic schooling course (GA 322).

Goethe wished to outline and survey the whole domain of physics. This overview aimed to show how we should approach all physical manifestations in a way that would correspond to his intentions as expressed in his treatise on colours. But of this survey the only part published concerned his theory of music, which arose from Goethe's conversations with Zelter.[63]

Here a question remains about Goethe's relationship with music theory. This is a rather complex matter, since we find here not one but two different sources for his ideas. In his correspondence with Zelter we learn various things about the mature Goethe's thoughts on music. But there are really two sources for this. One was his own somewhat naive musical understanding. He was not very diligent in his music lessons, and this may be because he wasn't exactly industrious in other areas of learning either if the teachers were somewhat dull. If we look, say, at Goethe's spelling at a certain age—we can see this in manuscripts from Goethe's archive around 1775, when he was already well into his twenties—we can be sure that a schoolteacher today would put red marks all over it, and say it was very sloppy work, very inadequate. So one source for his ideas on music was his naive response to music rather than any musical proficiency.

Then there is another source of his ideas on music; based on his treatise on colours he tries to gain a view which we could call a general theory of physics. This treatise on colours is a very original effort, isn't it, undertaken with huge inner industry and drawn entirely from its subject. But he was not able to embark on original investigations in all areas of physics. And so there is much in his views of music that developed by analogy with his treatise on colours. He therefore gave schematic outlines on music in which he attempted to find an analogy in music with what he experienced in the realm of colours, in light phenomena. And this is the second source of his ideas.

And now a third aspect—not a source, now, but a kind of approach to the subject—is added by virtue of the fact that Goethe had to the very greatest degree an instinctive sense of the paths we are now pursuing in spiritual-scientific enquiry. In a great many passages in Goethe's writings we can discern a remarkable, experiential awareness which comes to expression in all kinds of ways, sometimes theoretically as in the treatise on colours, sometimes by theoretical analogy as in his theory of music. But in poems, too, Goethe's lower soul reveals remarkable instinctive insights into the path and approach. Especially interesting in this respect are poems that remained fragments, such as his *Pandora*. If he had completed *Pandora*, it would have been a work written entirely out of the world of spirit. It would really have needed to be viewed in the world of spirit.

Now Goethe did not reach spiritual vision but inwardly he was entirely true. This is also why he did not complete the work; it stalled because of his inner weighing of things. To study how Goethe always stalled in such matters and then left them to one side because he was profoundly truthful in his nature is one of the most interesting things about Goethe's creative work and poetry. Here we see that Goethe's sensibility was approaching that of anthroposophy, the science of the spirit. And this was the third aspect. And so, through his genius, he did in fact perceive more in the world of tones than could have been expected from the musical instruction he had received.

But it was precisely this that helped him to overcome his prejudices, and gives his schematic presentation of music a certain spiritual-scientific air. His theories on music, for instance the polar relationships between major and minor, can of course be interpreted in the most diverse ways: they are just schematic, one thing running parallel to the other. So you see we need an intimate knowledge of Goethe if we wish to understand how he was thinking. And then there would be ways of arriving at very favourable results. In fact Goethe's theory of music could be of great interest for both a physicist and a musician. Goethe's scientific work is also imbued with an artistic element. In his schema on the theory of music we really do have something that strikes us like a kind of partitur: there is something musical in it; and likewise there is a musical quality in the way he presents his treatise on colours.

Try reading Goethe's theory of colours with an eye to its composition, the sequence of findings, the sequence in which he describes his experiments. I recommend that you do so. And afterwards try reading an ordinary book on physics—the section on optics in a modern book on physics. You will find a very great and significant difference; for a time will come when in relation to science, too, people will sense that they should consider the *how* more than the *what*. The *manner* of a scientific account is what really shows how we understand something. It is amongst the saddest developments today that the less artistically one writes the more highly one is regarded in the academic world. Naturally no one says this, but everything is geared to it. In later times, no doubt, some interesting cultural-historical reflections will be written on current barbarisms in scientific style—at present no one has an inkling of this. No doubt many pages will be devoted to a discussion of the 'stylistic barbarism in science in the nineteenth and twentieth centuries'—that is, if there are still old codgers who write as much about everything as old codgers do today.[64]

Steiner's intense preoccupation with the philosophy of Arthur Schopenhauer also falls in his Weimar period. In 1885 Cotta published Steiner's twelve-volume edition of the philosopher's complete works. In his detailed and differentiated reflections on Schopenhauer, whom he once called a 'narrow-minded genius'[65] *in a discussion with Otto Erich Hartleben, Steiner repeatedly refers—chiefly in his early lectures on music between 1905 and 1908—to the philosopher's belief that music is the art of the super-earthly, the world of the will.*

Schopenhauer is a nineteenth-century figure who introduced clear, apt ideas about art. He assigns music a very particular place amongst the arts, and art as such a very special value in human life. The basic stance of his philosophy was that life is an awkward business and that one could try to make it endurable by reflecting on it. In his view, an unconscious, blind will holds sway everywhere in the world. It forms the stone, and from the stone the plant, and so on, because it is always dissatisfied. In other words, in everything there lives a longing for a higher condition.

The human being himself feels this, although the greatest differences exist: someone of dull awareness is much less conscious of dissatisfied will than someone at a higher level, who senses the pain of existence much more clearly.

Schopenhauer says that besides the will we also have thinking. He calls it a 'fata Morgana', a fleeting, misty will-o'-the-wisp, or ripples on the surface of the will's dark, surging waves. In us, he says, the will raises itself into this illusory apparition of thinking, and when we see the will through it we become still more dissatisfied. But there are ways and means to release ourselves from the blind urge of the will, and one of these is art, through which we can lift ourselves beyond the will's dissatisfaction.

Whenever someone creates a work of art, he does so out of his thinking. But whereas other ideas are merely pictures, something else happens in art. For instance, the statue of Zeus by Phidias did not come about as a realistic representation of a person. Instead, the artist combined many impressions, retaining all virtues and merits in his memory and discarding all deficiencies. By combining the qualities of a great many people, he created an archetype that cannot be found in nature except in so far as it is distributed over many individuals. Schopenhauer says that the true artist reproduces archetypes rather than our ordinary ideas—not reflections or copies but archetypes—and by doing so, as it were plumbing the depths of creative nature, he finds redemption.

This, he says, is the case in all arts except music. The other arts have to pass through thinking, thus providing pictures of the will. But the musical tone is a direct expression of the will itself, without intrusion of thought. When we work artistically with music, it is as if our ear were pressed to the heart of nature itself; we hear the will of nature and reproduce it in a sequence of tones. Thus—says Schopenhauer—we can gain an intimate relationship with the 'things-in-themselves'; we penetrate into their inmost reality. Because we feel close to the essence of reality in music, it gives us a profound sense of pleasure and satisfaction.

In this way, out of an instinctive perception, Schopenhauer assigned to music the role of directly representing the nature of the cosmos. He possessed a kind of instinctive sense of the real circumstances. Why music can speak to all of us, why it affects us from the earliest infancy, becomes comprehensible in the realm of existence where music has its true origins.[66]

This view of music is rooted in ideas we encounter in Schopenhauer a long time before he became preoccupied with philosophy. When a commercial apprentice in Hamburg, he wrote to his mother:

How did the heavenly seed find space on our hard soil where necessity and dearth fight for every little corner? We have been banished by the primal spirit and must not reach to his lofty sphere . . . and yet a compassionate angel begged the heavenly flower for us, and it took root and unfolded into full glory on this soil of misery. The pulse of divine music has not ceased beating through all the centuries of barbarism, and a direct echo of the eternal has been preserved for us in it, understandable to all, and raised even above vice and virtue.

We encounter this idea again later in philosophical form in Schopenhauer's chief work.[67]

In Schopenhauer we can see Fichte's phrase most clearly confirmed—that the world-view we choose depends on what kind of person we are. Schopenhauer had difficult experiences in life, and was acquainted with the worst aspect of the world before he ever decided to reflect on it in philosophy. It satisfies him, therefore, to picture this world as inherently irrational, as the outcome of blind will. In his outlook, reason can have no sway over unreason; and this is because reason itself is the outcome of unreason, and is appearance and dream engendered by the will. Schopenhauer's world-view is the gloomy tenor of his sensibility transposed into thoughts. His eye was not intent on taking pleasure in reasonable modes of existence, for he could see only the sufferings and pain expressed by the unreason of blind will. His ethics could therefore only be based on a perception of suffering. An action, for him, is only moral if it is based on such perception. *Compassion*, he says, must be the source of human actions. Someone who perceives that all creatures suffer can do nothing better than allow compassion and sympathy to govern all his actions. Since unreason and evil lie in the will, a person will be all the more morally elevated the more he kills off impetuous will in himself. The expression of the will in an individual is self-seeking, egoism. But if we dedicate ourselves to compassion, exerting our will not for ourselves but for others, then we become master of it. One way to get free of the will is in dedication to artistic creativity and to the impressions we receive from works of art. The artist does not work because he wants something, because his self-seeking will is geared to things and processes, but he creates out of unegoistic joy. He immerses himself in the nature of things as a pure observer. The same is true when we enjoy works of art. If we are standing in front of a painting and feel a desire to own it, we are still enmeshed in the will's low desires. Only when we admire beauty without desiring to possess it have we raised ourselves to the sublime place where we are no longer dependent on the blind will. And then art becomes for us something that releases and redeems us for moments at a time from the blind unreason of will-driven existence. This release is purest in our enjoyment of the art of music. Unlike other art forms, music does not speak to us through our thinking or picturing. It does not copy anything in nature. Since all natural phenomena and processes are only thoughts and pictures, the arts that draw on them as their model can only approach us as representations and ideas. By contrast, we engender tones out of ourselves without a natural model. Since we possess the will in us as our intrinsic nature, the world of music can only emanate directly from the will, and this is why music speaks so strongly to our human sensibility: because it embodies and expresses our inmost nature, our true being, the will. And it is a human triumph that we possess an art in which we can selflessly and will-lessly enjoy the origin of all desire and all unreason.[68]

7. RUDOLF STEINER ON DIVERSE COMPOSERS

Rudolf Steiner closely followed developments in music in his day. He loved music and was a keen concert- and opera-goer, also valuing high-quality 'light' music such as Johann Strauss's Fledermaus. *Of the composers of his time he spoke most often about Richard Wagner, whose operas he attended in Vienna, Weimar, Bayreuth, Berlin and Stuttgart. Between 1905 and 1908 he gave around 20 lectures on Wagner's work, and in 1907 said that he was 'one of the greatest artists of modern times'.*

The public lecture which Steiner gave at the Architects' House in Berlin on 28 March 1907 sums up his views on Wagner and his work.

Reflections such as those we will undertake today, which connect Richard Wagner with mysticism, can easily awaken certain prejudices due to misunderstandings arising where one seeks to study an artist from a spiritual-scientific standpoint. Then there is also a second kind of prejudice encountered in regard to mysticism itself.

Everything I will say today about Richard Wagner's place in art on the one hand and mysticism on the other can appear contradictory, since I find a great deal in Wagner that he himself has never uttered or expressed. To counter such a prejudice it has to be said that the person engaging in these reflections has of course pondered this objection from the outset. But when we consider a spiritual phenomenon in the world, it is never enough simply to record what the person in question, in this case the artist, has himself said about it. If we were to abide by this principle it would be impossible ever to pursue observations of phenomena that take us to a genuinely higher realm.

No one after all would ever expect a botanist or a lyric poet to confine his descriptions of or, in the second case, his feelings about a plant to what the plant itself can utter. The words of the botanist or lyric poet are born from his soul. Whatever we say about any phenomenon in the world, spiritual or otherwise, cannot be expected to originate entirely in its own utterances. If this were so, the plant itself would have to be able to express the laws of its own growth and being, and the poet would be thought wrong to speak feelingly on behalf of a natural phenomenon without using its own words. But the opposite is true: in the human soul there must announce itself what the outer world cannot say about itself.

Please consider in this light everything that I will say today about the 'spiritual phenomenon' Richard Wagner. Just as the plant does not itself know the laws of its own growth, and yet still grows according to them, so an artist must not necessarily express the laws a spiritual scientist discovers in his whole being. Nevertheless the artist embodies the laws according to which he creates his works, just like the plant embodies laws that are only discovered in retrospect. The objection that Wagner himself has not said what I will say does not, therefore, hold up to inspection.

Then there is what is commonly called 'mysticism'. Scholars and lay people speak of mysticism as if it were a dark, nebulous way of thinking about the world compared with a scientific, conceptual approach. The Gnostics spoke of mysticism as 'mathesis', mathematics—not because mysticism is mathematics but because true mystics seek from higher worlds of spirit the same crystal-clear transparency and luminosity that, in another field, mathematical ideas and concepts also possess. When we rightly understand mysticism we find it to be not a dark, feeling mode of comprehension but the very clearest there can be: a crystal-clear insight into the world.

These two perspectives, therefore, which negate two prejudices, will inform what I will say today.

It is possible to consider Richard Wagner from the highest perspective. It can certainly be said of him that he was a seeker of the spirit who spent his whole life in the most authentic quest to discover the sources and foundations of universal enigmas. He called his house at Bayreuth 'Wahnfried' (meaning 'peace from delusions') and in doing so made clear that this was because he found rest there from illusory things. This name is really very significant.

Anyone who truthfully and honestly attempts to pursue a path of knowledge and who gives expression to the realms of spirit he believes he has discovered on his quest—in whatever form he does so, whether in art or in another form—knows what delusions can beset him on this path, hindrances of illusion. And he knows also that knowledge, insight, is not something that simply unfolds in a dry and prosaic way. He knows that insight is actually something that arrives amidst inner tumult and crisis, through inner ascent and collapse; he knows that this path is beset by terrible dangers on the one hand, and the possibility, on the other, of wonderful happiness and bliss. He knows that if he pursues this path of knowledge, there is a prospect of attaining peace, divine peace, which emerges from an intimate immersion in the divine secrets of the cosmos. Something of this outlook and this mood can be found in what Richard Wagner said about his home: 'Let this house be called "Wahnfried", for here my delusions gave way to peace.'

He was not an artist, like so many others, who sought to create his works out of fantasy devoid of substance, but rather one who from the very beginning regarded his calling as a great, world-historical mission. In his creative work he sought beauty that was at the same time truth, an elaboration of true insight. For him, religious sensibility was at the same time the soul of artistic creation. Being an artist was for him a priestly calling. What the artist Richard Wagner gave to humanity was at the same time intended to bear a religious, a sacred quality, as he saw it: to fulfil a religious task and mission in humanity's evolution. He felt himself to be one of those who wish to give their age something drawn from the depths and wealth of truth.

If the science of the spirit is not to be abstract, dry theory, nor to take flight into a cloud-cuckoo-land far removed from reality, it must find ways to understand and evaluate such a significant cultural phenomenon as Richard Wagner. Understood in the right way, it has the means to do so.

Richard Wagner bore within him a feeling and sensibility that led him towards the same truths about the sources of human evolution that spiritual science also discovers. There is something that deeply connects Wagner with spiritual-scientific sensibility, and with all true mysticism; and this is what he refers to as the harmony of the different arts, the unity of the arts—their harmonious and pleasing accord. He objected to the deficiency he identified in the arts in modern times: the self-seeking egoism at work in their separate fields. Instead of one art going in one direction and another in a different one, his ideal was to establish harmony and concord between them so that all could work together selflessly in loving dedication. In his view, such art had once existed, an artistic ideal of this kind, and was found in ancient Greek culture preceding the age of Sophocles, Euripides and others. Before the arts divided from each other, he said, with drama and dance going in different directions, they worked together and were united in a total work of art in one, selfless endeavour. He intuits this total work of art in a kind of clairvoyant vision. History does not record it, but we must nevertheless affirm his view since it looks back to the origin of diverse peoples where not only the arts worked together in great, united concord, but where all fields of culture and spirit altogether also collaborated.

What we call art and science today, spiritual science regards as branches that sprang from a single root. Whether we go back to ancient Greece or to ancient Egypt, India or Persia, or to the origins of German culture, everywhere we find an *ur*-culture inaccessible to materialistic enquiry but available to clairvoyant vision. We encounter a culture where science and art were not sundered, where all was united, and where everything tended to be seen as a wonder, a mystery. Before there were arts and science establishments there were mystery centres. What were they? A place where wisdom, beauty and religious piety were united.

We can form some idea of what occurred in those ancient temples, which were at the same time schools and true centres of artistic creation, if we conjure before us a sense of the great cosmic drama presented to those who were allowed entry to the ancient sacred places, the mysteries. As I said, materialistic history has nothing to report of such things. But someone who was allowed entry there could watch presentations of drama and music, infused with wisdom, and pervaded with things that elevated the soul to true religious piety. Through spiritual science we can picture what occurred on these occasions, though external records tell us nothing of them. Those gathered there could watch a kind of drama of the creation of the world—such Creation plays were very common. They depicted how primordial divine beings descended from heights of spirit and let their nature flow into the substance of the cosmos so that this was shaped to form the diverse beings of nature, the various kingdoms of nature: the mineral, plant and animal realm, and that of humankind. In these performances the divine was seen to flow down into the diverse beings of nature, and to celebrate a kind of resurrection in human souls.

In Egypt, in the Osiris drama, and in the various temple and mystery centres of Greece, was depicted something that deeper sensibilities have always felt: that the world has emanated from the divine, and in the human soul comes to awareness, as it were looking outward again through human eyes and senses and observing itself in its creative activity. The temple and mystery performances showed this descent and resurrection of the divine. Those who were allowed to watch them saw the whole of human art and wisdom combined to present this drama of the creation of the world, what we might call an *ur*-drama. And in watching it they felt, first and foremost, a religious mood. With awe and reverence they saw the god descending into matter, slumbering there in all beings and then resurrecting in the human soul. With deep veneration they felt a mood that Goethe once beautifully expressed in these words:

> When the healthy nature of the human being works as a whole, when he feels himself to live in the world as if within a great, beautiful, dignified and worthy totality,

> when harmonious contentment grants him a pure, free rapture, then the universe, if it could experience itself as having attained its goal, would rejoice and wonder at the summit of its own being and development.

Similarly, a wonderful religious mood poured into the hearts of those who watched this universal drama.

As well as this religious mood, there was also wisdom, embodied in all that human beings later formulated as scientific ideas about the world's origins and its creatures. This was made vivid for those watching: wisdom perceived in outward picture, and science that was at the same time religion. Since beauty was conveyed in outward pictures and images, and since the wisdom informing these performances gave rise to piety, such universal dramas were both science and art simultaneously.

The soul of Richard Wagner had dim inklings of this original harmony of the different disciplines. Naturally he looked back firstly to this *ur*-culture of ancient Greece, which still had a religious character; and he said that here music, drama, dance and architecture were not yet sundered and separate but, in the most ancient times, still all worked together as one: a unity of religion, art and science. And then, as Wagner saw it, the arts departed from this selflessness and became self-seeking and egoistic. Wagner had a great power of intuition and intimation. He looked back to the most ancient past when people were not yet so individualized as today, not yet as subjective and personal as they became. Individuals still felt themselves to be members of a community or tribe, of their whole nation or people. The folk spirit, the spirit of the tribe was still regarded as a reality. Wagner looked back to those ancient times of natural selflessness and this idea occurred to him: to become individual, people had to distance themselves from the old tribal communities and the personal element had to emerge as the sole basis for their incipient freedom. Freedom cannot be gained without a kind of egoism. Thus Richard Wagner looked back to all that had enabled people to cohere together. People had to distance themselves from this selfless state and become ever more conscious. This is how he saw the very ancient past. And then he saw that, having attained freedom, they must find their way back to fraternal bonds, to loving association with each other; and through consciousness the self-seeking human being must become selfless once more—love must again infuse all.

To him this appears as the ideal for art in the far future. The present here meets the future, with art having an important part to play in our further development. It seems to Wagner that art runs parallel with humanity's evolution. The arts have evolved alongside human beings. They emerged from a totality to become egoistic. Drama, architecture and dance as we know them today all became something separate. Going hand-in-hand with a world grown egoistic, we also have an egoistic art. Wagner looks forward to a time when art will again be integrated into a community of the arts; and this is why he calls the artist a 'communist' because he was thinking of a 'communism' of all artists. In this exemplary harmony of the arts, to which he wishes to contribute his own mite, he sees a means to pour into human souls the quality of selflessness that must serve as the foundation of a future human brotherhood. As an artist, therefore, he was a missionary of human social selflessness; he wished to pour into every human soul the impulse that will guide it towards inner selflessness so that humankind can be harmoniously united. This was a grandiose missionary idea that surfaced in Wagner's soul, one that could only dawn in someone, imbue someone entirely, who himself possessed something of a true, spiritual impulse, who cultivated a deep faith in the reality of the life of spirit. Richard Wagner did indeed possess this faith.

In Wagner's work *The Flying Dutchman*, we can begin to get a sense of this faith of his in the spiritual world behind the sense world. There, already, we find in Wagner a true and very honest faith in the spiritual world underlying sensory reality. Please remember that I am not in any way claiming that Wagner himself consciously entertained the thoughts I am expressing, just as little as the thoughts of the botanist or the poet live consciously in the plant. But in the same way that what the botanist or poet writes is drawn from it, so Richard Wagner lived in accordance with these ideas, with these spiritual laws.

Materialists see people all around them, and regard them as standing distinct and separate from each other in their material existence. The soul is enclosed in sensory bodies, and so the materialist believes that there is no other kind of community between people than the one mediated externally through the senses. An individual can only say or do something to another in a purely outward, materially real way: that is what the materialist thinks. But anyone who is aware of a world of spirit underlying the world of the senses is convinced that a hidden community exists between people, that something passes from one soul to the other even where there is no outward material influence through spoken communication or action. Hidden spiritual effects stream from soul to soul. What one person thinks and feels, even if this stays shut within his soul, is not insignificant and worthless for others to whom these thoughts and feelings relate. A materialist knows only that others can support him by material means. He does not believe that the feelings living in him have real importance for others, that souls are united by bonds invisible to the outward eye. The mystic knows that such bonds exist, and Wagner was profoundly imbued with the truth of this.

If we wish to understand what this signifies, we can look back to a lovely medieval legend—or rather something that people today regard as a legend but which for the author who wrote it and those who try to understand its mystical meaning is more than a legend, is the expression of a spiritual reality. A legend that figures in a medieval epic tells us of someone named 'Poor Henry' who had a terrible illness. Only one thing, we are told, can cure this illness, and that is if a pure woman sacrifices herself for him. The love of a pure feminine soul can thus be of real significance for another's life, and the whole legend is founded on the thought that souls can mean something for each other in a purely spiritual realm of which materialists have no idea. The sacrifice made by a pure, feminine soul for the sake of Poor Henry is surely, ultimately, nothing other than an expression or metaphor for what a large part of humanity regards as the mystical effect of sacrifice. This virgin's sacrifice for the sake of Poor Henry is surely what the Redeemer accomplished on the Cross, for the sake of humanity: the mystical, spiritual effect that passes between souls. We sense and intimate that behind external reality can live something spiritual in nature. And this is why Wagner drew upon the legend of the Flying Dutchman, a man so closely bound up with material reality that he cannot find any release from it, becomes entangled in it. There is good reason why the Flying Dutchman has been called the

Ahasuerus of the ocean, the wandering Jew of the sea. Just as something profound lies in the idea of the wandering Jew, so likewise there is deep meaning in the thought of the wandering Jew of the sea, the Flying Dutchman.

Let us consider Ahasuerus from this angle: he is someone who cannot believe in the Redeemer, a figure who leads humanity forward to ever greater heights, to increasingly evolving perfection. Ahasuerus is entangled in existence as it is. Whereas we must advance from stage to stage if we wish to progress, someone who lacks the will to strive for this can instead bind himself to matter. He can dismiss and disparage the one who guides humankind towards ever higher stages, and consequently becomes entangled in matter. What does this mean? If we are entangled in matter then external life endlessly recurs in the same uniform way. You see, the difference between material or spiritual comprehension is that the material way of life continually repeats itself whereas the spirit ascends. The moment that spirit succumbs to matter, it succumbs also to ongoing repetition of the same, and this is what happens to the Flying Ducthman. In olden times, diverse peoples were able to use their encounter with new, foreign lands to raise their ideas ever higher. Those who could do this regarded ocean voyages, the storming of foreign coasts, as merely a means to perfect themselves. But those who could not embrace this idea of self-perfection or the onward flow of spirit became entangled in the uniformity of what belongs solely to matter and substance. The Flying Dutchman, with his sole focus on material things, loses the powers of development, of love, which is the means to perfect oneself, to ascend, to evolve. Consequently he spins himself into matter, substance, so that everything simply repeats endlessly for him. Such natures who cannot find the impulse that raises them higher must be touched by a virginal nature. To release and redeem the Flying Dutchman, the other must be virginal and filled with pure love.

The soul who is not yet entangled in matter has a connection with the one who is. Richard Wagner senses this and expresses it in his drama in a very significant way, in a mystical feeling of truth, a feeling for the community of spirits that underlies the community of matter. Truly, someone who felt these things might claim for himself, as Wagner did, a lofty spiritual mission, might direct his winged thoughts into realms where he thought quite differently about music and drama than people had done before him. In his own way he looked back to early Greek culture where the arts were unified, where music only expressed what the rest of a drama could not fully bring to expression without it, where eternal laws of the universe came to expression in the rhythms of dance. In ancient art of this kind he found something where dance, rhythm and harmony were still interwoven and united in ancient musical-dramatic forms. And a singular view arose in him about the nature of music: he saw its essence in the harmony of tones; but he thought that only if the sister arts offer up to harmony what they have to give will something necessary flow into music. One of these sister arts is dance—not the dance that later came to human expression, but forms of dance which manifested movements in nature and the motions of the stars and planets. This was a more ancient dance form, which emerged from a feeling for natural laws so that the dancer's movements reflected what occurs, moves and unfolds in the natural world. This rhythmic dance infused musical harmony and endowed it with rhythm. And then the other sister art, poetry, was added. Originally it could only express a few things in words, and what the words could not express had to be conveyed by the other arts: so that dance, music and poetry worked together harmoniously, giving rise to the triad of harmony, rhythm and melody. The harmonious interplay of these three sister arts produced it.

The mystic perceived this to be the spirit of ancient art, before melody, rhythm and harmony had attained their later perfection. Richard Wagner is aware of this, as is the mystic. And now he said this: the arts that first worked together in sisterly fashion later grew separate. Dance and poetry became something distinct. Rhythmic experience grew to be a distinct domain, and likewise music, which no longer wished to know anything of its sister art. In the same way poetry was sundered from music, and no longer infused music with its element.

Richard Wagner saw that as human egoism increased, the arts also grew more egoistic, and he traced this development of the arts into the modern era. Here we cannot follow the whole course of development which he discovers as these arts grow ever more autonomous and egoistic. But let us consider his attempt to create something harmonious from the one-sided specialisms that have arisen. Here we discover the grandeur of his work in his efforts to fathom the underlying nature of these things.

Two figures stand out for Wagner: Beethoven and Shakespeare as representatives of the divided arts of music and drama. For Richard Wagner, the dramatic art of Shakespeare was one-sided. He had a deep, inner sense that the whole range of feelings and emotions cannot be expressed in words alone, cannot pass into gestures or even into words, and that therefore something essential is not conveyed. Dramatic words convey occurrences that have already emerged into space and time from inner impulses. As a drama unfolds we have to conclude that a protagonist has already experienced the impulses that now lead to his words and actions. Everything passes into what the eye can see and the ear can hear, rather than conveying the inner drama within someone. Thus the dramatist must be silent about the deeper underlying feelings and emotions that lead to outward actions and words on the stage.

On the other hand he also sees composers of purely instrumental music as one-sided. Through their wonderful configurations of tone they are able to represent what occurs within us, the inner drama; and yet this remains interior, without physical gesture, does not flow on into space and time. So we have the art of music which expresses our inner life, yet fails to convey it outwardly, and on the other hand dramatic art that has detached itself from its sister, music, and can only represent impulses that have already streamed into space and time. On the one hand Shakespeare and on the other Mozart, Haydn and Beethoven embody for Wagner two tendencies in art. In Beethoven's Ninth Symphony he sees something that is trying to break the confines of a one-sided art form, burst its bonds and come to expression in words because it seeks to encompass all humanity in love, because it is pushing its way out into the whole world. He sees something that seeks to emerge into space and time, and he sees his mission as carrying this still further into space and time: not only as the Ninth Symphony does this by giving utterance to feelings and allowing the soul's inner drama to stream out; not just as Beethoven does this, but he wishes to take this further into word and action so that both are present on the stage—the inner range of feelings in the music, and in the drama the outward actions drawn from these feelings, and entering space and time. Wagner wishes to reconcile

Shakespeare and Beethoven in a higher unity. He wishes to represent the whole human being.

When we see actions unfold on stage we should not just see what is revealed to our eyes and ears but also hearken to the inmost impulses at work in human beings. This is why old forms of operas were not enough for Wagner, for librettist and composer were still separate in them. The poet expressed what he had to say, and the musician joined forces with him to express the words. Yet music should exist to express what poetry cannot. The human being has an inner life that cannot come to expression in outer life, and an external aspect that can, certainly, be conveyed in words but falls silent about inner impulses. Music therefore should not simply illustrate poetry but complement and complete it. Music must express what poetry cannot.

This is Richard Wagner's great idea and the impetus for his creative work. He sees his mission as bringing music and poetry into selfless interplay in a total work of art. This founding idea really originates in a mystical source, one that seeks to encompass the whole human being—not just our outward life, but our permeation by interiority to create a whole. We are more than our outward expressions. Richard Wagner knows that within us dwells a higher self which only partly and partially appears and comes to expression in space and time. Richard Wagner wishes also to encompass this aspect of us that goes beyond the mundane and everyday; and this is why he resorts not to one means alone but to the diverse means that correspond to our whole being. He must resort to something that goes beyond our immediate personality, that raises itself to a level beyond the human. And this occurs in myth. In a mythical figure we encounter more than a separate individual: something superhuman. Myth expresses the meaning of the superhuman within us. Figures such as Siegfried and Lohengrin convey something that lives not in one but in many human beings. Wagner drew on the superhuman figures in mythology because he sought to fathom the deepest aspects of human nature.

We can see how deeply he engages with the whole process of development and evolution if we study his works a little. He raises himself to the highest human enigmas as these come to expression so magnificently in the Nibelungen and Parsifal dramas, and he seeks to elaborate them from a view, a feeling, a sense of the whole of humanity.

And now we can shed some light on what lies in Richard Wagner's artistic soul. We can see, from just a little study, how deeply connected he is with the mythical contexts in which humanity is embedded. Why exactly does Wagner reach for the story of Siegfried? What was he seeking to convey here? We can best understand this if we recall Wagner's idea of the whole course of human evolution. He looked back to primordial times when tribal people were closely bound together through an original, selfless love, when the individual was scarcely aware of being separate from others but instead felt himself first and foremost to be a member of the tribe, of the community to which he belonged, when he experienced something very real in the group soul of his people. Above all, Richard Wagner sensed how something that had lived in Europe led back to very ancient times when an original love still united people in brotherly groups and communities. He looked back to the times of which spiritual science speaks in its account of how consciousness gradually evolves. Our modern, clear awareness emerged from states of which only faint vestiges now remain. In dream consciousness, in dream pictures, Richard Wagner saw the echoes of a pictorial consciousness that the whole of humanity had once possessed. Today's waking consciousness, lasting from morning to night, until we fall asleep, has suppressed a much duller and more ancient kind of awareness in which people were far more closely connected. Back then the human individuality had not emerged so strongly, nor had the human egoism that accompanies this, which is a necessary stage in human evolution. Thus Wagner saw that a natural love once existed, born of blood ties and closely connecting all blood relations.

Now, drawing on rational mysticism, I wish to offer a view which for those of you who did not attend the other lectures may seem somewhat grotesque, but for the others will acquire a kind of mathematical assurance. What lives today in Europe as our modern waking consciousness evolved from a primordial form of humanity, the Atlantean condition, which preceded our own. This early form of humanity lived where the Atlantic Ocean's waves now roll. Those of you who keep up with current developments will know that an Atlantean continent figures even in mainstream science. An article about this appeared in the scientific journal *Kosmos*. The ancestors of the people who now inhabit Europe lived under different physical conditions in those times. They still lived in air and water. The ground was largely covered with great, thick swathes of mist. You could not see the sun in the same way as we do today: it was surrounded by great aureoles of colour. The world of Germanic myth and legend retains a memory of that ancient land in the expression 'Niflheim' or 'Nibelungenheim'. These are memories of that old land of mist; and a fine, intimate aspect of this legend, this memory of ancient days is that as the floods gradually covered the land of Atlantis the same waters also formed the rivers of the

German lowlands. And so the Rhine is regarded as a remnant of the Atlantean mists that once covered the land far and wide. It is as if the waters of the Rhine had condensed from the thick mists of ancient Atlantis, the 'Nebelheim' or 'home of the mist'. The legend thus offers a dim intimation of this. And as the peoples moved eastwards, having to leave because of physical circumstances, they also left behind them this dim form of consciousness. Their awareness grew ever brighter and more awake, and at the same time egoism increased.

Ancient, dim consciousness gave rise to a certain selflessness. As the air cleared, egoism dawned. The mist and fog of ancient Atlantis created around the human being an atmosphere of wisdom that was filled with selflessness and love. This flowed into the waters of the Rhine and rested there, below its surface, as wisdom, as gold. But when egoism encompasses this it gives rise to egoistic power. Thus as the representatives of the ancient inhabitants of Nibelungenheim moved eastwards they saw the Rhine enclose within it the hoard of wisdom's gold which had once been active in a selfless way. All this resided, though not expressed in this way, in the world of legend of which Richard Wagner's soul took possession. And this soul of his was in such concord with the great spiritual being working in these legends, and retaining a memory of the old realities, that he could draw forth an essence of its whole world-view. In the music of Richard Wagner, therefore, we hear echoes, and see dramatic representations, of the growth and action of human egoism. We see the fashioning of the ring after Alberich takes the gold from the Rhine, from the nymph of the waves. We see in Alberich a representative, grown egoistic, of the Nibelungen. We see the human being who has abjured the love that places us into a whole context and community. The power of possession is something Wagner connects with the idea living in that world of legend. This is how he sees that ancient world, the world that founded Valhalla: the world of Wotan, of the old gods. These have something that all human beings once had in common. They embody a kind of group soul, as does Wotan. But where the ring takes hold of a single individual, and encircles the human I, he is at the same time gripped by lust for gold. And so Richard Wagner's whole art, all his works, convey a fine sense of what lived as group soul in Wotan, as well as the human being's egoistical experiences of the Rhine gold. We hear this resound in the tones of his music. Is there anyone who does not sense this? No one should think that he simply imposes something on his work. I object strongly to such a suggestion. Who does not sense the influx of the I in the E flat major passage in *Rhinegold*? How should the human ear not sense the appearance of the I in this long, held tone of the E flat major passage in *Rhinegold*?

Thus we have been able to trace Richard Wagner's mystical feeling right into his art of music.

Then we see how Wotan must grapple not with the consciousness that has been woven from soul to soul, but—where a living sense of folk consciousness still lived—with what has not yet been spun forth. This consciousness appears where Wotan seeks to take the ring from the giant. The old consciousness rises before him there in the figure of Erda. The words spoken here are important. Would anyone dispute that this figure is invoked as a representative of the old consciousness, who does not only know what reason connects, but also knows, through clairvoyant awareness, what occurs in the wider world of nature?

To you is known
What the deeps harbour,
What lives and weaves
Through mountain and valley
Where beings are
Your breath doth blow
Where minds reflect
Your senses cling
Everything, it is said
Is known to you.

One cannot more clearly invoke the ancient consciousness that existed in Nebelheim than with these words:

My sleep is dreaming
My dreaming is reflecting
My reflecting is the sway of knowledge.

Thus it was: a consciousness like dreaming, but one that was aware of the whole environment. This played between people, and worked into the deepest depths of nature. This was the human being's reflecting, will, his actions, for he acted out of this consciousness. It was this consciousness that appeared before Wotan in Erda, and this gave rise to a new consciousness.

In all mysticism the higher element is embodied in a female figure. This is present too in Goethe's beautiful words in the Chorus mysticus: 'The eternal feminine draws us ever onward and upward.' Diverse peoples have represented this striving for a higher consciousness as union with a feminine quality that embodies the higher aspect of the human soul. The soul is irradiated by universal laws, with which it unites as in a marriage. Thus you see how a higher state of soul awareness is depicted as feminine, in a way that corresponds to the character of each people—for instance, Isis in ancient Egypt. What a people feels to be its true essence is represented as the connection with a particular feminine figure, either at death or already in life.

As these lectures have already shown us, we can grow beyond our sensory nature in two ways. Firstly we can shed the 'skin' of sensory life and unite with the spirit at death, or secondly we can do this already during life if we open our eye of spirit. Accordingly we see how this higher nature that we can experience is also depicted as a feminine figure in German myth. Our central European ancestors saw themselves as warriors who fight bravely and, falling on the field of battle, encounter the Valkyries who bear them upwards into the world of spirit. The feminine figures of the Valkyries represent a connection with higher consciousness. With Erda, Wotan fathers Brunhilde, with whom Siegfried must unite if he is to find his way to spiritual life. The daughters of Erda represent the initiate's higher consciousness. In Siegfried the new human being matures; the distinctive nature and perfection of his inner qualities enable him to unite with the Valkyries already during life.

Richard Wagner gave expression to qualities that live in the world of German legend. He also invoked the fact that the ancient group soul must die away in a twilight of the gods, just as individual consciousness must come to the fore in Siegfried. All these things were living and working in his soul. The highest problems of humanity lived and worked within him; in so far as they depict the inner life of human beings he embodied them in music, and in so far as they embody human deeds he depicted them in dramatic form.

Thus we see how, as artist, Richard Wagner draws the

human being's higher development from a mystical realm. This led him to conjure a deeply significant figure as the centre of his dramas—the figure of Lohengrin. Who is this? We only understand this figure if we see how the legend becomes important during a time of major social upheavals in Europe. Then we can see what is living in the soul of Wagner as he portrays Lohengrin in his union with Elsa, Duchess of Brabant. We see how a new age is approaching throughout Europe—an age in which the struggles of the human individual are coming to the fore. We can express this in a seemingly very prosaic way, and yet it conceals something of great profundity. In France, Scotland, England and further away in Russia we see a new social configuration arising: the free state. Whereas country folk everywhere are still living in the fading echoes of an old sense of community, those who wish to detach themselves from this more tribal sense of belonging leave the country for the cities. Here, in the city, a sense of individual freedom was dawning, and here lived those who wished to pull themselves free from communal bonds, and sought to live singly and alone. This was a huge change from the past. Until then a person's name told you where he belonged and what his standing was. In the city this name became a worthless thing. Who cared now which family you had grown up in? A person was worth only as much as his abilities. The individual developed. The development from selflessness to individuality led on then from individuality to fraternal association, to the 'band of brothers'. In the middle of medieval times, the legend represented this, as the old was replaced by what a person could make of himself from within.

If we look back to the ruling priestly sects of ancient times, to those who once governed and embodied a 'wise nobility', we find that they belonged to family groupings. It was important in those times that they possessed the right blood lineage. In the future this will no longer be important. Leaders of humanity can now arise from unknown quarters, and giving them a 'name' will be a kind of profanity. Instead, the nameless figure of wisdom is increasingly emerging as an ideal of great individuals. Nameless men or women of wisdom do not become something important through their ancestry but through what they are in themselves. This is the free individual whom others acknowledge because he draws from himself all that he is and can be for others. Thus Lohengrin stands as representative of this quality, as a leader of humanity towards freedom. We see medieval city consciousness embodied in the woman who unites with Lohengrin. The figure who stands between humanity and the great beings, who mediates humanity's dialogue with the great leaders of humanity, is shown to unite with one of humanity's great individuals. Such a figure has always born a particular name—in all occult and esoteric science this figure is referred to as 'the swan'. The swan is a very specific level of higher spiritual development, uniting the ordinary human being with the higher guide and leader of humanity. We see a reflection of this in the legend of Lohengrin.

Such things do not have to be formulated in a strict and pedantic way—that would be wrong. We only gain clarity if our concepts become broad and open-hearted so that the things which Wagner conveys to us are not pedantic word-husks but instead kindle ideas that can continually be developed and enlarged. Allow me to present you with concepts that are not confined within pedantic contours but instead open far perspectives. One has to see a figure such as that of Lohengrin in its whole world-historical significance, recognizing how understanding of this evolved in Richard Wagner's soul and assumed an artistic form.

The same was true of Wagner's approach to the legend of the Holy Grail. In our last lecture 'Who Are the Rosicrucians?' we engaged with this idea of the Holy Grail. It is very remarkable that at a certain moment a kind of intimation of that great medieval teaching of the Holy Grail shone forth in Richard Wagner's soul. It first dawns in him as another thought fades. In 1856 an idea emerged in Wagner's soul that he intended portraying in the drama 'The Victors'. He never executed this; but what he wished to infuse into it came to expression in *Parsifal* instead. The nature of the earlier idea can become apparent if we study his drafts and plans for 'The Victors'.

Ananda is loved by a Chandala girl (an 'untouchable'), but the caste prejudice means he is far removed from being available for this love: he may not accept it. He conquers his own nature by becoming a pupil of the Buddha. In this discipleship he finds victory, regains himself, overcomes human desires; it is revealed to the Chandala girl that in a former life she was a girl of the Brahmin caste and rejected the love of a Chandala youth. She too becomes victorious through this knowledge, and is united in spirit with Ananda, the Brahmin youth.

Wagner expresses this all in a beautiful way, bringing it close to anthroposophic, Christian foundations of reincarnation and karma. We are led to the point where the girl, in her former life, has inflicted upon herself what she now experiences. Wagner already developed this in 1856.

On Good Friday 1857, Wagner was sitting in a lonely hut, his 'refuge on the green hill', looking out over the fields and seeing new green growth emerging from the ground. He had a sense suddenly of the forces of growth that the sun entices from the earth and which pervade the whole world—an intimation of the driving force that lives in every creature but cannot simply remain as it is. If this is to rise to ever higher spheres, it must pass through death. This is what he felt as he observed the sprouting, burgeoning plant world while looking out over the Lake of Zurich and Villa Wesendonck: the polar idea, the opposite, that of death—the same thought that Goethe expressed so beautifully in the phrase that concludes his poem 'Bliss of Longing':

> And as long as you fail to possess
> This dying and becoming, growth and dearth
> You will remain a cheerless guest
> Upon the dark globe of this earth.

He rewrote this as the hymn to nature to express how nature invented death because it desired to have more life: a higher, spiritual life that it can only create out of death.

This is what Richard Wagner felt and experienced on Good Friday, when the symbol of death appears before humanity to remind us of this. He sensed the connection between death, life and immortality. He directed his feelings from the life that sprouts forth from the earth to the death on the Cross, which is at the same time the great source of Christianity's faith that life will vanquish death and attain to eternal life. The life of eternity springs from this death. The deep affinity between the idea of Good Friday, the idea of redemption, and the sprouting, burgeoning life of nature lived in Richard Wagner; and this idea is identical with that of the Grail as we described it, where the chaste plant with its flower strives sunwards in contrast to the human being with all his desires. He saw the human being filled with appetites and pondered on the ideal of the future when, through overcoming our desire nature, we will have attained a higher consciousness, a higher, fertilizing power that will generate the spirit. And he looked towards the Cross, seeing how the blood of the Redeemer flowed and was caught in the Grail vessel, giving rise to the symbol for this idea of redemption; and for him this became connected with the growth of nature. In 1857 this idea suffused Wagner's soul, and he briefly recorded in writing what he subsequently invoked in his magical portrayal of Good Friday. He wrote: 'From death the growing world of plants, and in death eternal life for the Christian.' He felt here the spirit underlying all things, and the spirit as victor over death.

This idea of *Parsifal* remained for a while in the background, while he attended to other artistic ideas; but at the end of his life it emerged and came into ever clearer focus for him as a picture of the human path of knowledge. This led him to depict the path to the Holy Grail, to show how the human being's desire nature can be purified. This ideal is depicted in the pure, sacred vessel which represents the plant's calyx: through the sun's ray, the sacred love lance, it is fertilized to give rise to pure, chaste new creative activity. The sun's ray penetrates substance as the lance of Amfortas penetrates sinful blood. There, however, it causes suffering and death. If this sinful blood is cleansed so that it becomes as pure, at a higher level, as the flower calyx, this appears as the path to the Holy Grail, which can only be found by one who, with pure heart, and untouched by worldly things, without worldly knowledge and living in his quest for the secret of the world pursues it as a 'pure fool'.

Thus we see how the *Parsifal* idea is born in Richard Wagner out of mystical depths from the idea of the Holy

Grail. He had intended to portray this by presenting the whole of medieval history, a kind of historical drama, in his work *The Wibelungen*. The medieval idea of the emperor was to be spiritualized by making Barbarossa ride to the Orient; and he wished to show all Indian culture streaming into the outward empire, and within it the original spiritual element of Christianity that the hero was seeking. And so, for Wagner, this idea of medieval stories about the emperor pours into the Parzival legend; and in the idea of *Parsifal* he was then able to give such wonderful artistic expression to Christianity's tradition of Good Friday that, as I see it, he really accomplished the ideal that had been in his mind, that of making art religious. In this artistic reshaping of the Good Friday tradition, Richard Wagner gave expression to that fine and brilliant idea of the interplay of the themes of faith and the Grail: the idea that humanity will be redeemed, that we will gradually be perfected as we strive towards redemption, that in Christ Jesus as Redeemer is luminously prefigured what streams through humanity as the spirit, a drop of which every soul possesses as its higher self.

On Good Friday 1857 this already stood before the soul of Richard Wagner: an intimation of the connection between the *Parsifal* idea and the Redemption by Christ Jesus who pervades the spiritul atmosphere in which humanity lives, and whom we can sense if we enquire feelingly into the tale of the Holy Grail. This can reawaken to a tangible life of spirit and soul as, in the idea of Good Friday, we draw forth again a feeling for the transition from midnight on Maundy Thursday, from the departing world of Maundy Thursday, to Good Friday as the symbol of the victory of resurrecting nature.

Something else that lived in Wagner as he drew forth his

work of art from a direct apprehension of this festive idea was a sense of the need to revitalize the festivals. The festivals are born from a living understanding of nature. The Easter festival was established at a time when people knew that the constellations of sun and moon work into human minds from the natural world. This comes to tangible expression in the festival of Easter. People today want to determine things in abstract ways, no longer experiencing things as they did when they were intimately conversant with nature. If one has a spiritual sense of things then one experiences everything around one spiritually. If we can still sense what tradition has handed down to us in the form of festivals, then we will also feel something that Good Friday should give us. Richard Wagner sensed this, and also felt the significance of the Redeemer's words, 'I am with you to the end of the world,' as an exhortation to follow the signs that can lead us to the high ideal of the Holy Grail. Then human beings who live in truth will become redeemers themselves. A Redeemer brought salvation to humanity. But Richard Wagner went further and asked, 'When will the Redeemer be redeemed?' He will be when he lives in every human heart. Just as he has descended into every human heart, so every human heart must ascend to him. And of this too Richard Wagner had a sense as, out of the motif of faith, he gave utterance to humanity's mystic intimations in the beautiful final words of *Parsifal*:

> Miracle of the highest salvation:
> Redemption for the Redeemer!

These words show him to be truly united and at one with the highest ideal a human being can have: to approach the power that lives in the world and seeks to descend to us. If we endeavour to become worthy of it then we bring what sounds forth at the end of Wagner's *Parsifal*—redemption for the Redeemer.[69]

In the first half of his life, especially, Rudolf Steiner greatly esteemed the music of Beethoven. In a questionnaire sent round literary circles in Weimar in 1892, he wrote that Beethoven was his 'favourite composer'.[70] Yet his writings and lectures make no reference to Beethoven. But we do have a note of a conversation he had with the pianist Walter Rummel (1887–1953) about Beethoven's outstanding importance. To Rummel's question about the 'mission of Beethoven's symphonies', Steiner replied:

His music prepares the human being's higher bodies; this is something humankind must first learn through music.[71]

The dimension of this answer can remind us of the effect of music as preparation for logical thinking by the Bodhisattva Apollo in the third cultural epoch.[72]

Before the turn of the twentieth century, Rudolf Steiner met some of the composers of his generation in Vienna and Weimar, and wrote some aphoristic reminiscences about them. In his later Vienna period, at the home of the writer and women's rights advocate Rosa Mayreder, he met Hugo Wolff (1860–1903) and described this composer of numerous song cycles as follows:

At Rosa Mayreder's house I often took part in conversations involving creative individuals who gathered there. Hugo Wolff, a close friend of Rosa Mayreder, would sit there quietly, apparently looking inwards more than attending to what was happening around him. Though he spoke very little, one's soul attended to him. What he experienced was mysteriously communicated to those who shared his company.[73]

Steiner encountered Gustav Mahler (1860–1911) during the 30th composers' gathering of the German Music Association in Weimar, where, on 3 June 1894, Mahler conducted his first symphony, which at that time was still entitled 'Titan'.

Mahler was there for instance, in his early days, as director of a music festival. The way he moved his baton made an unforgettable impression: not commanding music's flow of forms, but pointing meaningfully *between* its forms in a way that conveyed the experience of a concealed supersensible element.[74]

In his Weimar Period, Rudolf Steiner often encountered Richard Strauss (1864–1949).

In Weimar at that time, Richard Strauss was taking the first steps in his career, and working as deputy director of music alongside Lassen. Strauss's first compositions were performed in Weimar. This composer's musical endeavours struck one as intrinsic to the cultural life of Weimar itself. Such a joyful and devoted absorption of something that, in the process, became a lively artistic problem was only possible in the Weimar of that time. All around dwelt the calm, worthy composure of tradition—and now into this erupts Richard Strauss's tone poem *Also sprach Zarathustra*, or even his Eulenspiegel music. Everything wakens from its sleep of tradition, but does so in a way that attracts pleasant affirmation or no more than gentle dismissal; and thus, in the finest way, the composer is able to find his relationship to his own creative work.

For many hours we sat and listened to the first performance of Richard Strauss's musical drama *Guntram*. Heinrich Zeller, such a likeable, fine and humane person, sang the main role and almost lost his voice in doing so.[75]

Steiner's acquaintance with Strauss in Weimar led to a joint event for the poet John Henry Mackay at the National Theatre in Berlin. Steiner gave a lecture about the latter's work. Strauss accompanied his wife, the soprano Pauline Strauss-de Ahna, on the piano in his own compositions of Mackay's poems.

Rudolf Steiner felt that his own views of music had a close affinity with those of the Vienna composer Josef Matthias Hauer (1883–1959), whose stance was diametrically opposed to that of Arnold Schoenberg's 12-tone music. It seems unlikely that he met Hauer on the occasions when he came to Vienna, but he studied the latter's book, Interpretation of the Melos *which was published in 1923, and spoke at length about Hauer and his outlook when giving the Tone Eurythmy Course in February 1924.*

While speaking to you about tone eurythmy, I have been thinking often of a really very important modern Austrian musician [. . .] who was born in Vienna's New Town and with great vehemence has opposed the whole trend in modern music—which he refers to as 'bad European music'. He is an interesting phenomenon, one that should particularly interest eurythmists. Hauer learned music very young, starting from the age of five or so; in particular he learned to play the zither and got a long way with it, and gained the view that it is a very easy thing really to acquire skills involved in 'modern music'. One can tell from Hauer's whole manner that he is in certain respects extraordinarily honest inwardly. What is today called music is something he thinks can very easily be acquired, but considers that the truly musical element is lacking in this—that engaging with it actually distances us from music as such. Much of what I said about eurythmy's expression of music features in a blatant and radical way in Hauer's views. For instance, he speaks of atonal music. I have said that the real element of music, its spirit, lies between the tones, in the intervals—in what one does not hear. Hauer speaks of atonal music, and in doing so touches on something very true. He considers that the struck tone, the resonating harmony contains merely a sensory impulse, merely a help by means of which the inaudible melos, which constitutes the inmost human soul, can come to outer expression.

In our modern culture and civilization, especially as far as the arts are concerned, there is something so decadent and chaotic that we can easily warm to someone who, with a certain brilliant panache, states that modern music is just noise really, and not music, and fathoms what music is really founded on. We can well understand if such a figure feels real fury about the state of affairs, and directs this fury at all European artists today. This is the case with Hauer.

[. . .] I have been interested in Hauer for a long time now. In trying to lead music into the art of eurythmy, I had to enquire into various things that Hauer says; and I concluded that actually one cannot develop his atonal melos into the gestures of eurythmy. This won't lead us to eurythmy gestures. And I asked myself why this was so. He feels the movement of the melos with such inwardness, sees with such clarity what is important in music—so why does this not lead us into eurythmy gestures? There is a very simple explanation for this. Hauer hates the civilization that lies at the foundations of European culture, and which the rest of humanity admires so greatly—he hates ancient Greek culture. He is someone who has an excessive hatred of Greek culture.

Now it is interesting to get to know someone like this who genuinely and honestly hates Greek culture. There are plenty of people, in fact, who dishonestly worship Greek culture, although many are also honest in their regard for it. It goes without saying today that people revere Sophocles and Aeschylus. It is an interesting phenomenon to find someone berating these figures as the despoilers of art, and we should pause for thought and examine it. Hauer berates them because, in his view, they made all art into spectacle, and everything audible into visible form. Well, ultimately this is true. It is just a matter of knowing whether one can also love what is tangible and visible. If we seek to develop eurythmy, we must of course love the visible. If we do not love what is visible, if we do not genuinely love it, and wish to go no further than what is audible, the melos, then we will never embrace the Greeks as those who made everything tangible and visible.

Amongst the Orientals were inspired individuals who did actually seek to hearken to the audible. They had an architecture which was, basically, music in space. Oriental architecture contains a great deal of eurythmy. We can see the melos here pouring itself out into movement. Europe had little understanding for a musical architecture as this manifested here at the Goetheanum, for this was basically a kind of rejection of Greek architecture. The Goetheanum had little of Greek architecture in it; but it was both musical and eurythmical.

Now you see, this is why Hauer hates speech since it goes beyond melos [...]; really it violates it, pushes it outwards into externality. The moment we speak and give ourselves up to what the meaning of speech sounds demands of us, we become unmusical in a sense. Speech sounds, speaking verbal utterances, is an art which only faintly invokes the melos. The melos can peer through speech, as it were, but cannot be elaborated there. You cannot form words so that the vowels in them could really be thirds or similar, in the schema I established here. You can't do this—the world won't allow it. The world will not for example allow this: when, let's say you feel a sense of wonder, an *ah*, you cannot immediately afterwards express a feeling which creates the interval of a third with the feeling before. That's not possible, is it? Life continually destroys the aspect of music. This is why nature is unmusical, and why we cannot draw music from nature.[76]

For further study of the themes in this book I recommend the volume of Steiner's lectures on music, edited by Helmut von Wartburg (GA 283, 4th edition 1989, not currently available in English). This contains eight lectures, two answers to questions from the first anthroposophic School course, as well as two concluding addresses following lectures by the instrument maker Franz Thomastik and the composer Leopold van der Pals. The appendix to this volume also has notes by Mathilde Scholl and an index of comments on music by Steiner, drawn both from his written works and his lectures.

Reading and study are of course only one aspect of a deeper engagement with music. The other is actual, tangible experience of the single tone, the melos, time signatures and much more. Heiner Ruland's book Expanding Tonal Awareness *(Rudolf Steiner Press, 2014) is a very useful guide to this practical, experiential approach.*

NOTES

GA numbers refer to German editions of Steiner's work

1. Lecture on 23 February 1924, GA 278, p. 71.
2. Cited in: Volker Hage, Georg Hensel (eds.), *Indiskrete Antworten. Der Fragebogen des F.A.Z. Magazins*, Stuttgart 1985, pp. 18f.
3. See for instance Manfred Spitzer, *Musik im Kopf*, Stuttgart/ New York 2002; Hans Günther Bastian, *Musik (erziehung) und ihre Wirkung. Eine Langzeitstudie an Berliner Grundschulen*, 4th edition, Mainz 2012.
4. Lecture of 23 August 1921 in GA 77b, pp. 43f (German edition). See chapter 2, page 35.
5. See chapter 4, p. 53.
6. See Heiner Ruland, *Expanding Tonal Awareness: Musical Exploration of the Evolution of Consciousness Guided by the Monochord*, Rudolf Steiner Press, 2014.
7. See Armin Husemann, *Der hörende Mensch und die Wirklichkeit der Musik*, Stuttgart 2010.
8. See chapter 6, p. 147.
9. *Des A.M.S. Boethius fünf Bücher über die Musik*, translated into German by O. Paul, Leipzig 1872.
10. GA 9, pp. 122–4.
11. Lecture of 13 September 1907, GA 101, pp. 150–3.
12. Lecture of 11 June 1910, GA 121, pp. 93f.
13. Lecture of 11 June 1908, GA 102, pp. 221–3.
14. Lecture of 2 May 1923, GA 224, p. 36.
15. Lecture of 3 November 1912, GA 140, pp. 74–6.
16. Lectures of 19 and 26 February 1918, GA 277a, p. 112.
17. Lecture of 16 March 1908, GA 102, pp. 89f.
18. Lecture of 17 March 1908, GA 98, p. 215.

19. Lecture of 12 August 1908, GA 105, pp. 140–2.
20. Lecture of 18 December 1921, GA 209, pp. 111f., 115.
21. Lecture of 15 April 1924, GA 309, pp. 47–9.
22. Lecture of 29 December 1914, GA 275, pp. 47–53.
23. Lecture of 1 February 1924, GA 234, pp. 80f.
24. Lecture of 2 June 1923, GA 291, p. 173.
25. Lecture of 23 August 1921, GA 77b, pp. 43f.
26. Lecture of 23 August 1920, GA 201, p. 111.
27. Lecture of 26 February 1924, GA 278, pp. 99–106.
28. Lecture of 2 May 1923, GA 224, pp. 35–8.
29. Lecture of 12 September 1920, GA 271, p. 198.
30. Lecture of 3 December 1906, GA 283, pp. 11, 13–18.
31. Lecture of 30 December 1914, GA 275, pp. 60–4.
32. See chapter 4.
33. The three weeks of what became known as the first course of the School of Spiritual Science, lasting from 26 September to 16 October 1920, were accompanied by numerous artistic performances and over 90 lectures on a range of specialist themes. Paul Baumann's lectures were published under the title 'Music and the Art of Eurythmy in Education' in Eugen Kolisko (ed.): *Aenigmatisches aus Kunst und Wissenschaft. Anthroposophische Hochschulkurse*, Stuttgart 1922, pp. 331–56. The opening and closing addresses by Rudolf Steiner have not yet been published in the Collected Works but were printed in the first edition, 1928, of *The Art of Recitation and Declamation*. The main course was published in GA 322, the four medical lectures in GA 314, and three lectures on the art of speech and drama in GA 281. The latter, along with three further lectures on the Goetheanum building and its architectural principles (first printed separately in 1942) are planned for inclusion in GA 288.
34. Lecture of 29 September 1920, GA 283, p. 47.
35. Ibid. pp. 48–53.
36. Lecture of 30 September 1920, GA 283, pp. 75f.

37. Lecture of 9 January 1915, GA 161, p. 23.
38. Lecture of 8 March 1923, GA 283, pp. 146f.
39. Lecture of 2 December 1922, GA 283, pp. 101–16.
40. Lecture of 22 August 1924, GA 243, pp. 232–6.
41. In: *Bilder okkulter Siegel und Säulen*, GA 284, p. 95.
42. Lecture of 1 January 1915, GA 275, pp. 99f, 104–8.
43. Lecture of 20 February 1924, GA 278, pp. 38, 41.
44. Lecture of 25 February 1924, GA 278, p. 98.
45. Lecture of 7 March 1923, GA 283, pp. 123–30.
46. Lecture of 8 March 1923, GA 283, pp. 133–47.
47. Lecture of 16 March 1923, GA 283, pp. 159–63.
48. GA 21, p. 152.
49. Lecture of 7 March 1923, GA 283, pp. 121–3.
50. Lecture of 17 December 1920, GA 202, pp. 172f.
51. See *The Merchant of Venice*, Act V, Scene 1.
52. Lecture of 16 September 1920, GA 302a, pp. 35f.
53. Lecture of 14 June 1908, GA 98, p. 247.
54. Lecture of 25 October 1909, GA 116, pp. 24–9.
55. Lecture of 1 June 1918, GA 271, pp. 175–9.
56. Volume V in Kuerschner's *Deutsche National-Literatur.*
57. Lecture of 9 November 1888, GA 271, pp. 32f.
58. See the reprint in GA 1e, pp. 596–600.
59. Johann Wolfgang Goethe, *Sprüche in Prosa*, quoted in GA 1e, p. 501.
60. Ibid. pp. 501f.
61. Ibid. p. 502.
62. Ibid. footnote, p. 501.
63. Ibid. footnote, p. 596.
64. Questions and answers on 30 December 1920, evening, GA 283, pp. 77–80.
65. See Rudolf Steiner, *Mein Lebensgang* ['Autobiography'] GA 28, pp. 232f.
66. Lecture of 3 December 1906, GA 283, pp. 11–13.
67. GA 33, p. 256.

68. GA 18, pp. 273–5.
69. Lecture of 28 March 1907, GA 55, pp. 207–39.
70. Cited in: Volker Hage, Georg Hensel (eds.), *Indiskrete Antworten. Der Fragebogen des F.A.Z. Magazins*, Stuttgart 1985, pp. 18f.
71. Unpublished entry in the diary of Friedrich Husemann, *c.* 1958, Armin Husemann Archive.
72. See chapter 5, p. 136.
73. GA 28, p. 160.
74. GA 28, p. 278.
75. GA 28, pp. 276f.
76. Lecture of 23 February 1924, GA 278, pp. 71–4.

SOURCES

The following volumes are cited in this book. Where relevant, published editions of equivalent English translations are indicated. The works of Rudolf Steiner are listed with the volume numbers of the complete works in German, the *Gesamtausgabe* (GA), as published by Rudolf Steiner Verlag, Dornach, Switzerland.

RSP = Rudolf Steiner Press, UK
AP / SB = Anthroposophic Press / SteinerBooks, USA

GA	
1	*Nature's Open Secret* (AP)
9	*Theosophy* (RSP / SB)
18	*Riddles of Philosophy* (SB)
28	*Autobiography* (SB)
33	*Biographien und biographische Skizzen 1894–1905*
55	*Supersensible Knowledge* (AP)
77b	*Kunst und Anthroposophie. Der Goetheanum-Impuls*
98	*Natur- und Geistwesen—ihr wirken in unserer sichtbaren Welt*
101	*Mythen und Sagen. Okkulte Zeichen und Symbole*
102	*Das Hereinwirken geistiger Wesenheiten in den Menschen*
105	*Universe, Earth and Man* (RSP)
116	*The Christ Impulse* (RSP)
121	*Mission of the Folk Souls* (RSP)
140	*Okkulte Untersuchungen über das Leben zwischen Tod und neuer Geburt*
161	*Wege der geistigen Erkenntnis und der Erneuerung künstlerischer Weltanschauung*
201	*Mystery of the Universe* (RSP)
202	*Universal Spirituality* (RSP)
209	*Nordische und mitteleuropäische Geistimpulse*

224 *Die menschliche Seele in ihrem Zusammenhang mit göttlich-geistigen Individualitäten*
234 *Anthroposophy and the Inner Life* (RSP)
243 *True and False Paths in Spiritual Investigation* (RSP)
271 *Kunst und Kunsterkenntnis*
275 *Art as Seen In the Light of Mystery Wisdom* (RSP)
277a *Eurythmy: Its Birth and Development* (Anastasi)
278 *Eurythmy as Visible Music* (RSP)
283 *Das Wesen des Musikalischen und das Tonerlebnis im Menschen*
284 *Rosicrucianism Renewed, The Unity of Art, Science and Religion. The Theosophical Congress of Whitsun 1907* (SB)
291 *Colour* (RSP)
302a *Erziehung und Unterricht aus Menschenerkenntnis*
309 *Roots of Education* (SB)

All English-language titles are available via Rudolf Steiner Press, UK (www.rudolfsteinerpress.com) or SteinerBooks, USA (www.steinerbooks.org)